Publications of the

CENTER FOR EDUCATION IN AFRICA
INSTITUTE OF INTERNATIONAL STUDIES

Teachers College, Columbia University

David G. Scanlon and L. Gray Cowan, editors

Language, Schools, and Government in Cameroon
HUGH O. H. VERNON-JACKSON

Divergence in Educational Development:
The Case of Kenya and Uganda
SHELDON G. WEEKS

Political Socialization in the New Nations of Africa
PENELOPE ROACH

Educating the Bureaucracy in a New Polity
TAMAR GOLAN

"Education for Self-Reliance" in Tanzania
(A Study of Its Vocational Aspects)
WILLIAM A. DODD

The Development of Education in East Africa
JOHN CAMERON

The Cost of Learning: The Politics
of Primary Education in Kenya
L. GRAY COWAN

Traditional Ethiopian Church Education
ALAKA I. KALEWOLD

Children in Africa:
A Review of Psychological Research
JUDITH L. EVANS

Essays in the History of African Education
VINCENT M. BATTLE AND CHARLES H. LYONS, EDITORS

Studying
School Children
in Uganda

Four Reports of Exploratory Research

MILLIE ALMY

JOEL R. DAVITZ

MARY ALICE WHITE

Center for Education in Africa
Institute of International Studies
Teachers College, Columbia University

TEACHERS COLLEGE PRESS
Teachers College, Columbia University
New York, New York

© 1970 by Teachers College, Columbia University
Library of Congress Catalog Card Number: 74-122748

Manufactured in the United States of America

Preface

Education is viewed in most African countries as a major vehicle for development. But education takes place within the mainstream of African society: social, political, and economic conditions profoundly affect the development and direction of African education. For solutions to many problems educators in Africa have been turning to the social sciences and history, as monographs in this series have already indicated. Yet another dimension to the problems of education in Africa relates them to the specific culturally conditioned learning abilities of African children. Knowledge in this dimension is needed so that curricula may be better adapted and teachers better trained to relate Western learning to the experience of growing up in still largely non-Western societies. For the gathering of this knowledge we must turn to the field of psychology.

This monograph and its companion volume, the bibliography by Judith L. Evans, are the first two works in psychology to be published in the monograph series of the Center for Education in Africa. The studies by Almy, Davitz, and White are the results of the Child Growth and Development Project of Summer 1967, sponsored by the National Institute of Education at Makerere University College, Kampala, Uganda, and funded by the Center for Education in Africa, Institute of International Studies, of Teachers College, Columbia University.

These studies are significant not only as a contribution to the growing body of literature on African psychology; they represent an effort to involve African school personnel in the collection of the data, so that the research will be of immediate benefit to African teachers and pupils. Thus the authors are able to make recommendations both for further research and for ways that African educators can effectively participate in this research. The Child Growth and Development Project was a pilot project, limited by the funds available and the time the researchers could devote to it. It is hoped that the means may soon be found to continue this work.

David G. Scanlon
L. Gray Cowan

v

Introduction

There is general questioning as to whether curriculum and teaching methods in the primary schools of most African countries are sufficiently related to the environmental and cultural background and the individual characteristics and interests of the children. For years educators in Africa have been emphasizing the crying need for psychological investigation and research with particular focus on African children—on how they learn and how they behave in their cultural setting. The urgent need for such studies has been discussed at various conferences dealing with education in Africa, and repeated recommendations for various types of child study have been made. But until the summer of 1967 very little by way of concrete study of the African child—of his abilities, interests, values, motivation, and aspirations—had been carried out in East Africa.

In 1967, with the encouragement of the National Institute of Education, Makerere University College, a team of three eminent psychologists—Professors Millie Almy, Joel Davitz, and Mary Alice White—from Teachers College, Columbia University, came to Uganda to initiate short-term exploratory research in three areas of African growth and development. Their reports of this research constitute the present monograph.

These studies, while significant in themselves, are perhaps more important for sensitizing afresh all who hope to influence the progressive development of education in Africa to the imperative need for more information on the behavior and growth of African children. This monograph represents a definite beginning. The Makerere staff and local teachers who worked with the Teachers College experts are maintaining a continuing interest in these studies, and it is expected that they will carry out follow-up work, digging more deeply into the psychological surface that has been hardly scratched.

Sound programs of education in East Africa cannot be founded simply on hypothetical assumptions or on the continued interpolation of data derived from children who live in other cultural worlds. On-going, long-term coordinated programs of research must be established to provide a framework of knowledge on which to build school curricula that are meaningful in East Africa. Hopefully, the work started at Makerere and the information contained in this report will inspire new studies. The need is immediate and too clear to require lengthy elaboration here. A sound system of education must be based on a sound psychological foundation.

To all who participated in the project, the Institute is very grateful. In particular, I want to thank Professor David G. Scanlon, Director of the Center for Education in Africa, Teachers College, Columbia University, for his pioneering support of the project. My thanks go also to Professors Almy, Davitz, and White for their professional contributions and for the personal stimulation they injected into our Institute community life. Others who provided invaluable assistance include Dr. Carl J. Manone, Chief of Party, Teacher Education in East Africa Project, and Mrs. Judith L. Evans, the coordinator of the summer project. To all these, and indeed to all the Headmasters, staffs, and children of the schools that participated so willingly in the project, I am very grateful.

W. Senteza Kajubi
Director, National Institute of Education
Makerere University College

Contents

I The Usefulness of Piagetian Methods for Studying Primary School Children in Uganda

MILLIE ALMY

The purpose of this research[1] was to evaluate the usefulness of methods and concepts derived from the work of Jean Piaget in the investigation of cognitive processes among primary school children in Uganda. The study and the recommendations for further experimentation presented here are based on two major assumptions.

The first assumption is that the kinds of thinking appraised by Piagetian techniques represent basic mental abilities that are essential to understanding an increasingly technological world. Related to this is the idea that these abilities come into being as the child matures and has experiences that confront him with certain ways of classifying and ordering objects and events. There is presumably, for each child, an optimum time for providing such experience. If that time is missed, teaching him more complex mathematical and scientific concepts may take much longer and be much less effective. For example, a child who fails to grasp the basic concepts of number in the early years of primary school can be expected to have increasing difficulty in the later years, no matter how much he is drilled.

To match instruction to the developing abilities of individual children is a goal yet to be realized in most classrooms where the numbers are small, let alone those where the class size runs to forty or more. Yet some appraisal of where some of the children in a classroom are in their thinking should be useful in teaching. The Piagetian kind of appraisal seems particularly valuable in getting behind the verbal facade that so often masks failures in comprehension.

A second assumption is that the techniques of Piaget's "clinical" interviews can be adapted so as to provide both normative information about the level of the children's thinking and information that can be used rather immediately and directly by their teachers. There is, however, little point in detecting a particular way of viewing the world, or in unmasking confusion, without also trying to ascertain its sources. The concepts that the child encounters in school, and the kinds of thinking expected from him there,

1

may or may not build on his out-of-school experiences. Accordingly, it seems important also to study the latter. What aspects of the world, what objects and events, have been made meaningful to the child, in his home and family? What patterns of thought has he acquired there? What kinds of problems has he learned to solve? Answers to questions such as these go beyond the Piagetian interviews into the cultural setting from which the child comes.

The work completed in the summer project reported here is not extensive enough to test the validity of these assumptions, but it does suggest the direction that further study and experimentation might take in order to do so. As the study stands, it may be regarded as a beginning for the eventual collection of normative data. It has made relatively little progress in exploring the feasibility of the teacher's use of information derived from Piagetian interviews in his classroom instruction, although it raises many questions in this regard. It also opens many avenues of inquiry regarding the ways in which cultural setting affects the child's thinking, both before and after he enters school, but provides no data on these matters.

THE THEORIES AND METHODS OF PIAGET

For some forty years, the Swiss psychologist Jean Piaget, initially trained as a zoologist and particularly interested in epistemology and logic, has been studying the thinking of children. Although the greater part of his research has been with children ranging in age from four or five years to eleven or twelve, he has also studied infants and adolescents up to the age of sixteen. Since so many aspects of the present study are derived from the theory and method of Piaget, brief comment on these seems in order.

A pervasive question in Piaget's work has been: "How does the ability to think logically and systematically and to deal with abstract propositions, as well as with concrete realities, evolve?" Interviewing children of varying ages, posing them many sorts of problems often involving ingenious demonstration and experimentation designed to test the stability of their concepts, Piaget has traced the sequences in which various concepts of the physical world, such as number and quantity, space and geometry, develop.

Of late, Piaget and his colleague Barbel Inhelder have pulled together a number of studies done over the last twenty years.[2] These describe the steps involved as the child moves from a state of thought where each moment of experience appears to be relatively unrelated to previous moments toward a state in which there is evidence of systematization of experience. In the latter state a true concept of logical class emerges. Initially the child becomes aware that objects and events can be categorized according to their similarities. Gradually he can identify the properties or characteristics that mark an object or event as a member of a particular class. He begins to recognize the extent to which objects or events can differ and still be counted in the class. He comes to realize that objects and events can be classified in different ways depending on the property under consideration. Eventually he grasps the hierarchical nature of classes.

These studies of classification, together with the earlier studies of the development of number and quantity, highlight the differences between the thinking of the older child or adult and that of the younger child. While the child of age four, five, or six may have great verbal facility, in that he knows many words and uses them fluently, he often attaches to them quite different meanings from those intended by adults and older children. His thinking, at this level, may be described as dominated by his perception, that is, by the immediate appearance of objects and events.

The classic illustrations of this tendency to be more perceptual than conceptual are seen in the various "conservation" experiments. In these the child, having agreed that two balls of clay, or two sets of identical objects, or two quantities of liquid, are the "same" or "equal," changes his view and asserts that there is more clay, or there are more objects, or there is more liquid, when he perceives that the shape of the clay is changed, the objects are spread over a larger space, or the liquid is poured into a differently shaped container.

Until the child is able to "conserve," that is, to bear in mind whatever aspects of an object or phenomenon remain the same while other aspects undergo a change in appearance, he is not likely to grasp many kinds of verbal instruction. He can learn to count and to recite the multiplication tables, but as long as he has no notion that the number of ten objects is the same regardless of whether they are arranged in two sets of five or five sets of two, or spread over the surface of a table or bunched together in a pile, he will have difficulty in reasoning systematically, and in following adult reasoning.

Piaget's reports of his studies of Swiss children have maintained that the basic concepts of number and an understanding of hierarchical classification emerge in a predictable sequence. Studies of American and European children in general support Piaget's findings, although the age norms are not always equivalent and the close relationship he postulates among the emerging concepts is not always verified.

The predictability of the sequence has suggested that the school curriculum might well be organized accordingly. In the United States and in England, curriculum revision has in a number of instances drawn on the work of Piaget.

On the other hand, the finding that there is considerable variation in the ages at which children acquire certain concepts, depending on cultural differences, individual experiences and, presumably, differential rates of maturation, has suggested that Piaget's techniques might be used to appraise the progress of individual children, and in the light of that progress to provide experiences designed to facilitate conceptual development.

Piaget has argued against the notion, subscribed to by some American educators and psychologists, that intellectual development can, by proper intervention, be greatly accelerated in the early preschool years. Nevertheless his theories clearly suggest, as do longitudinal studies of development such as those recently reviewed by Bloom,[3] that the nature of experience in the years before a child is seven is an important determinant of later ability to profit from instruction.

The present study can make no pretense of investigating the early experiences of children in Kampala. But it does constitute a beginning effort to examine some of the ways of thinking, or of viewing their world, that are characteristic of the children in the Primary-1 classes in two Kampala schools.

BACKGROUND AND PROCEDURES OF THE STUDY

Most of the study was completed in six weeks during June and July, 1967. Important preparations were, however, made in advance by members of the Institute of Education staff at Makerere. They gained approval of the Ministry of Education and secured the cooperation of the headmasters of the primary schools from which the children in the study were drawn. Members of the staff also reviewed several interview schedules that had been used in the United States and in Nigeria. Translations from English into Luganda of what appeared to be the most appropriate of these were begun prior to my arrival in Kampala.

An investigator who has the temerity to attempt the collection of data in a country with which he has had no previous contact, and in a language of which he knows not a word, is, of necessity, completely dependent on the competence, good will, and integrity of his informants. Whatever confidence I have in the data collected derives largely from my confidence in the two students who assisted me. Both are experienced teachers in primary schools, one having taught at the P-1 level. Both are Baganda, so Luganda is their first language, and both are fluent in English.

That we were able to move so quickly into actual data collection can also be attributed to the assistance provided us by Mrs. Judith Evans, the administrative coordinator for the Child Growth and Development Project. She was engaged in a study of children's sorting abilities and arranged for me to accompany her when she and a Muganda informant interviewed children in their homes and in schools. This experience provided an invaluable background for the present study. It also suggested some of the content to be included in the interviews.

Development of the Interview Schedule

In reviewing the various interview schedules sent them, and in submitting the proposal for the study to the Ministry of Education, the staff of the

Institute indicated that the present study would replicate Piagetian studies carried on in Nigeria.[4] As the interview schedule finally evolved, it included some tasks that were replications of some of those used in Nigeria and in the United States, some that were modified from the Nigerian study, and others that were specially designed for the present study.

Conservation Tasks. These three tasks replicate those reported in our monograph *Young Children's Thinking.*[5] Originally used with 300 kindergarten and first- and second-grade children in the United States, and currently in use in a three-year longitudinal study involving another 500 children, these tasks were also used in the Nigerian study.

The procedure for administering these three tasks is standardized.[6] The first task poses to the child the problem of "conserving" the equality of two sets of eleven objects (buttons) through two transformations in appearance. The second task deals with the conservation of the number of one set of buttons through two transformations. The third task concerns the conservation of the equality of amounts of water through one transformation.

To avoid giving the child verbal clues that would incline him to respond as he thinks the adult wants rather than to give his own spontaneous views, the child is led through an orientation procedure in which an open-ended question is introduced. In this procedure, the child makes comparisons between sets of buttons or between two quantities of water, when they are clearly equal and when they are unequal (for example, eight buttons and eleven buttons, and glasses that are two-thirds and one-third full). Once he has correctly used a phrase to indicate that the quantities compared are "the same" or that one has "more" than the other, the question posed for the next comparison is "What about now?" In the ensuing test situations, the number and amounts are equal but the configurations are changed. In each instance the child is asked to tell why he thinks the number or quantity has changed or remains the same.

Classification Tasks. The first set of these, involving beans, beads, and buttons, resembles some of the sorting tasks described by Inhelder and Piaget in *The Early Growth of Logic.*[7] With the possible exception of the last task, all of them involve perceptual matching and do not demand that the child function on a conceptual level. In the Nigerian study, similar procedures but different objects were used. A class inclusion problem—where a total class (beans) might be compared with subclasses (red beans, white beans, and so on)—was also included. Almost none of the Nigerian children in the five-to-eight-year age range was able to solve it. Similarly, only the rare first-grader and relatively few second-graders in the United States understood this kind of problem. Since it appeared that it would be equally difficult for children in Kampala, it was omitted from the present study.

For the first set of classification tasks (sorting), the child is presented with this collection of objects: three buttons—one red, one tan, one black; twelve beans—four red, two tan, two black, four green; eight beads (seeds of the sort that are strung on necklaces and worn by women in Uganda)—four green, in a shade resembling that of the green beans, and four black, similar to the black beads. The child is asked to put together the objects that are alike. After he has sorted, he is asked to tell how the objects in the groups he has made are alike. Three tasks designed to check the stability or flexibility of his groupings follow. In each he is given another object and asked where it shall be put. The first object is a button—larger than the others but resembling the green beans in color. The second and third objects are necklaces—one of black, and one of green, corresponding to the beads already sorted.

The second set of classification tasks (cloth similarities) also involves perceptual matching. The child is asked to indicate which of two pieces of cloth is like a third and to tell why. Some of the tasks permit him to match on the basis of color or form as represented in design, some on the basis of color or geometric form. The first five tasks involved plain colored cloth and cloth cut from the Kitenge printed material from which women in Uganda customarily make their dresses (the designs are stylized, representing forms—leaves and flowers, for example—encountered in nature). The remaining tasks involved geometric forms—circles, rectangles, and triangles—cut from plain red or blue cloth.

These tasks were developed after the research assistants had indicated that tasks involving geometric form discrimination would be difficult for Baganda children. (There are no words in Luganda for the precise description of squares, circles, and triangles.) They also noted that the children were both familiar with, and interested in, intricate designs and would have no difficulty in matching them.

In the first five tasks the child chooses the two pieces that he regards as alike from a set that includes two figured pieces of material with similar designs but different background colors and a single piece of material in a plain color corresponding to the background of one of the other pieces. The assumption is that a choice of the two figured pieces involves attention to form, while the choice of the plain piece and the figured piece of similar background color involves attention to color. Some attempt was made to see that colors were of similar intensity, that the pieces were of similar size, and that the presentation varied so that the piece to be matched was sometimes plain, sometimes figured.

The next three tasks resemble the classic tasks used to investigate color or form preference. In these tasks the child is, for example, shown a red rectangle and a blue circle of similar size. He is then given a blue rectangle. If he matches it with the blue circle, his choice appears to be based on color; if with the red rectangle, on form.

In a final task only one color, red, was used. The forms were two rectangles and a circle, with the rectangles differing in size.

The reader will note that only rudimentary attempts were made to vary form and color systematically and that there was no control over other related variables. The intent was to explore a method, not to gather data comparable to those obtained in color—form experiments in the United States.

Both in the tasks involving cloth similarities and in the sorting tasks, "test" questions were sometimes posed to the children. If, for example, a child showed no inclination to group objects other than on the basis of close similarity or identity (for example, the red button clearly separated from red beans, and also from the other buttons), he might be shown another grouping, told that "another child" had arranged them that way, and asked whether the other child was right or wrong, and why. In the cloth similarities tasks, a child consistently choosing on the basis of color would be shown a form choice, supposedly made by another child, and would be queried regarding its correctness.

The use of this method of inquiry renders the data from the classification tasks less comparable from child to child than would otherwise be the case. The method does, however, provide some interesting insights, since the child's justifications of his own or "another child's" choice reveals something of his ability to shift from one property to another in considering a sorting or matching task. In any future experimentation, similar "test" questions should be built into the procedure. Justification questions of this sort are, it may be noted, always included in the clinical procedures used by Piaget.

Seriation Tasks. The materials for these tasks consist of six cardboard strips, 4 inches wide and varying in length from 4 to 14 inches, on each of which is sketched a stick figure of a woman, and six corresponding cardboard strips, varying in length from 1½ to 4 inches, on each of which is sketched a basket. The child is asked to place the "women" in order from the biggest to the smallest. If necessary he is assisted. Then he is asked to order the "baskets" from the biggest to the smallest, giving the biggest "basket" to the biggest "woman", and so on. Finally, the interviewer interchanges the third and fourth "baskets," asking the child to show him the women whose baskets have been moved.

These tasks, similar to those used in the Nigerian study, were included at the urging of the research assistants, who thought that the children should have an opportunity to reveal their abilities in handling differences as well as similarities. Piaget maintains that the ability to order on the basis of differences, like the ability to sort on the basis of similarities, is an important forerunner of the conservation of number. Children's performances in seriation tasks of the complexity of those typically used by Piaget are difficult to record adequately and cumbersome to score. The task developed here is somewhat simpler than those used by Piaget, and does not get at the child's ability to handle ordinal numbers.

Direction Tasks. These tasks were developed by Miss Nakkazi, whose experience in P-1 suggested that the children would be readily able to discriminate on the basis of direction. The material for these tasks consists of four strips of cardboard, 4 inches wide and 25 inches long. On each strip is a set of line drawings, similar except for the direction in which they are oriented: seven flowers—three growing upward, four downward; five cups—two with handles to the left, three with handles at the right; four hens—two facing left, two facing right; seven men—three facing forward, two walking to the left, two to the right. Each strip is presented separately and the interviewer asks the child to tell him about it. If no mention of direction is made, the child is queried more specifically.

Translation of Interview Schedule

The conservation sections of the interview schedule were translated into Luganda directly from the schedule used in the United States. Two modifications were made later. In the section on conservation of an amount of liquid, the interviewers emphasized that the glasses into which the water was poured were identical. The child was also asked to pour the water from the glass into the bowl. In the earlier study this had been done by the interviewer. The other sections of the interview were translated as they had been developed.

All translations were discussed, and the appropriate words to use were agreed upon by the two research assistants. When the schedule was completed in Luganda, it was translated back into English by a research assistant[8] who had not previously shared in the discussion. This resulted in two changes. A term implying that the child should count was eliminated from the orientation section on the conservation of number. A term connoting "heaps" or "piles" rather than "bundles" was used in the sorting tasks.

During the course of the study, several individuals with a knowledge of Luganda, including the assistant who made the independent translation into English, observed the interviews and checked on the fidelity of the instructions to the children.

Training of the Interviewers

The procedures of the interview were role-played several times in English. Then five American children in a primary school where English is used for all instruction were interviewed by the two research assistants in English. Needed corrections were made, partly at my suggestion but largely through the assistants' evaluation of one another's procedures.

The Subjects

The primary school in Uganda has a seven-year program, with classes designated according to year; P-1, P-2, and so on. The majority of schools are operated by religious bodies, as were the two schools involved in this study, and financially aided by the government. There is no compulsory education law, and since financial resources are limited, fees ranging from 20 to 60 shillings per year are charged. It is estimated that about 60 per cent of the children in the primary school age group are in school. The age at which children enter school varies from six (or, as we found in a very few instances, five) to eight.

The 44 P-1 subjects in this study were drawn from the classes in two primary schools (Makerere Hill and Kibuli) where Luganda is used for instruction at the early levels. In the school where the interviewing began, the first children were selected by the teacher. The sample was later rounded out by including children of the required age or sex as they came on the register. In the second school, where there was a preponderance of girls, every third girl and every second boy were chosen from the register.

To provide some notion of the direction the children's performances in the various tasks might take as they grow older, 20 children in P-3 were also interviewed. Every other child on the register in one of the P-3 classes at Makerere Hill Primary School (there is no streaming at this level) was included. The interview procedures were identical with those used in P-1 except that the tasks involving direction were eliminated.

The researcher who is accustomed to getting information about the child's date of birth, the occupation and education of the child's parents, and his status on some kind of IQ test (whether or not he makes use of this information) confronts two problems when he comes to work in a country other than his own. One problem is to decide what information is really relevant to the study he is making. The other is to ascertain what information can readily be obtained. In the Nigerian study, through careful counseling with the teachers and the parents of the children, Dr. Etuk was able to secure information regarding not only the education and occupation of the parents but also the nature of the child's out-of-school activities and the extent of play materials, if any, in his home. Birth dates in Nigeria, as in Uganda, could often only be approximated.

In the present study, the ages of the children were taken from the school records. Information regarding parental occupation and language spoken at home was secured from the children where possible. In a few instances, where it was obvious to the interviewers that the child did not speak Luganda at home, the child was eliminated from the study.

Analysis of the Data

The children's performances in the conservation tasks were categorized according to the scheme set forth in *Young Children's Thinking.*[9] The categories for performance in the classification and sorting tasks were developed from inspection of the data. In the seriation tasks, credit was given for each correct performance. No attempt was made to evaluate the extent of the errors made when the performance was not correct. In the direction tasks, credit was given when the child correctly and spontaneously indicated all of the directions.

Some minor difficulties were encountered in the process of categorization. The recording of the children's responses was not always as complete as one would have liked. Since the recording was in English rather than in Luganda, the recorder sometimes imposed his own category system on the child's response, rather than recording it verbatim. This difficulty could have been eliminated had the categorization schemes been applied to an early sample of interviews so that both interviewers and recorders would have had a clearer understanding of the information needed.

More and earlier practice in the use of a categorization scheme presumably would have developed readier understanding of the necessity for certain arbitrary decisions. It might also have prevented a tendency toward confusion of the procedures used in categorization with procedures for scoring. Ultimately each member of the research team categorized each protocol and any disagreements were resolved by discussion.

RESULTS OF THE STUDY

Since the study was exploratory, investigating the possibilities for the use of Piagetian techniques, the questions that arose and the problems that were encountered assume equal importance with the findings regarding the children's performances in the various tasks. The sample of children interviewed is small, and it is representative only of the two schools involved. The validity of the data is dependent not only on the adequacy of the translation of the interview schedule but also on the ability of the interviewers to communicate with the children and to record their responses accurately. Any findings must be taken tentatively. Nevertheless, certain developmental trends are apparent and suggest that the children did understand what was expected and responded in accord with their own ways of viewing the world.

For a researcher lacking in cross-cultural experience, the children's behavior in the interviews was much more striking in its similarity to that observed among American children than in its differences. Initially, in each school, the children seemed, not only to the American observer but also to the other interviewers, to be somewhat restrained and lacking in spontaneity. Once the procedures got under way, with each child calling the next one from the classroom, the earlier reticence was less apparent. One noted a considerable range of individuality in the responses, some children offering spontaneous comments, others limiting themselves to answering specific questions. Although many of the children could be described as "shy" in the presence of two adults (sometimes three), almost none of them were evasive. The hanging head, the refusal to try, the whispered "I don't know" that had been observed among some groups of American children in similar situations were rarely encountered here. One suspects that these children have early learned to try to conform to adult expectations.

The children handled the materials, estimating the amount of water in a glass, pouring and re-pouring to get the levels to correspond, arranging the objects in the sorting tasks in precise lines and piles, in almost precisely the same ways as American first-graders. The explanations they gave in the conservation tasks, calling attention to the height of the water in the glass, or to the width of the bowl, noting that the buttons were bunched or spread, sometimes contradicting one observation with another, were also strikingly like those given by American children. When they were able to conserve, as some of the P-3 children were, the explanations they gave were as matter-of-fact and direct as those expected from American children.

There was one way in which the responses of the Kampala children did differ strikingly from the responses of their American counterparts. This was in the conservation tasks in which they did not conserve. American children tend to specify "more red" or "more yellow," "more in the glass" or "more in the bowl." The Kampala children tended to say only that things were "not the same." Whether this difference is genuine or spurious (resulting from the way the responses were translated) is uncertain. However, it underlines the importance, for future work, of recording the children's responses verbatim, in their own language.

It should be noted that the primary intent of this study was not cross-cultural. It attempted, rather, to appraise the ways the children in P-1 view certain situations, to find out what they spontaneously attend to, and to ascertain developmental trends by comparing their responses with those of P-3 children in the same situations. The five kinds of tasks that were used in the study constitute only a minute sample of the possible tasks that might be used to appraise children's thinking. Only the conservation tasks are exact replications of tasks that have been used elsewhere. As the following summary of the results indicates, several of the tasks have promising possibilities for further study.

Conservation Tasks. During the course of the interviewing, it was readily apparent that few of the P-1 children had yet developed a stable concept of number. Most of them were readily misled by a change in the appearance of a number of objects or a quantity of liquid. Applying the strict categorization scheme described in *Young Children's Thinking,*[10] credit for conservation could be given to only 30 children in the counting task, 8 children in the number task, and 5 children in the amount-of-liquid task. Since considerable uncertainty was involved in translation and in the fact that the children were not accustomed to being interviewed, it seemed fair to look for any evidence of conservation rather than adhere to a more stringent procedure. Children who give such evidence may, in Piaget's terms, be transitional: without a stable number concept but having a glimmering awareness of the possibility. Table 2 shows for each of the tasks the number of children in P-1 and P-3 who gave at least one indication that they understood that the number of buttons (or the amount of water) remained unchanged despite the transformations in appearance.

Table 2 highlights the importance of counting for these children. It also raises questions about the rapidity of development of the number concept. As in previous studies, it is clear that the counting task is the easiest and the task involving the amount of liquid the most difficult.

The children counted quickly and accurately. However, when the buttons they had just counted were spread apart, and the question "How many now?" was posed, most of the children attempted to count again. It was only with the second posing of the question, after the same set of buttons had been bunched, that they seemed to grasp the fact that they need not count again to be able to tell the number.

When the P-3 children are compared with the P-1 children, some progress toward a more stable number concept is apparent, but the contrasts between the two groups are not as great as one might anticipate from Piaget's research and various replications of it, which found conservation of number typically achieved in the years between seven and nine.

The lack of very striking differences between the P-1 and P-3 groups may reflect inadequacies in the mathematics curriculum, or it may stem from inadequacies in the interviewing procedure. Confronted with more tasks, and given more opportunities to justify their answers, it may be that the older children would have revealed more advanced thinking.

Classification Tasks. In both the sorting of objects and the selection of cloth similarities, the children had the option of paying attention to color or focusing on form. A number of children, apparently either preoccupied with differences or unable to distinguish the similarities in color or form, did not sort as anticipated or said that neither of two pieces of cloth was like a third.

The children's performances in the sorting tasks show clear developmental trends. Such trends are not apparent in their performances in the cloth similarities tasks. The data from both kinds of tasks were analyzed in terms of the supposed ages of the children and in terms of their level in school.

The data suggest that regardless of age or school level, color was more often than form the basis for sorting. However, in some cases children apparently accepted neither color nor form as a basis for sorting. They either made what Piaget terms "graphic collections," arranging the objects in lines or piles without apparent regard for either form or color, or sorted by putting together only those objects that were ostensibly identical. In the latter instance, the child would have nine "collections": four of beans, two of beads, and each of the three buttons placed separately. When a child who sorted like this was asked where the green button and the green and black bead necklaces should be placed, he would keep them separate from any other beads or buttons. In the cloth similarities tasks, such a child would maintain that a comparison sample was not like either of the pieces of cloth he was first shown.

In the course of the four sorting tasks, each child had 14 opportunities to group on the basis of either color or form. Not every child used all these opportunities. To determine the extent to which a child preferred color, the number of times he used color was compared with the total of his color and form choices. For example, a child using form 5 times and color 5 times has a total of 10 color and form choices. The proportion of his color responses to his total color and form responses is .50. Table 3 shows the numbers of children in each of the age groups according to the proportion of color responses made. It appears that for at least a quarter of the children at both school levels, form is a more salient property than color, at least in these tasks. But the predominant inclination, perhaps increasing with age, is toward color. This finding is in accord with other studies of African children.[11]

Some children never made a sort that could be characterized as based on either color or form, and some children made relatively few such sorts. Table 4 shows the distribution of such instances. Observation of the P-1 children in the interviews suggested that these children were more concerned with differences than with similarities and alert to any detail which made an object unique. The fact that 95 per cent of the P-3 children sorted consistently on the basis of color or form suggests that the apparent preoccupation of the younger children with differences is an indication of their lesser maturity. Other studies have indicated that attention to detail developmentally precedes awareness of similarity.

Table 5 shows the children's performances in a fifth sorting task, calling on them to place the previously sorted beans, beads, and buttons into *two* piles—one containing "things we can eat" and the other "things we cannot eat." Performance in this task, which is more conceptual in nature than the other four sorting tasks, is better in the P-3 group than in P-1. It is interesting, however, that a considerable number of the P-3 children, as well as of the younger children, refused to make one pile of the beads and buttons. One child asserted that it would be improper to do so since the buttons were "more useful" than the beads.

Table 6 shows the proportion of color responses given in the cloth similarities tasks, and Table 7 the number of times when neither color nor form was chosen in these tasks. As in the sorting tasks, a preference for color over form is apparent at both levels. There is also a slight indication that as the children grow older they are less inclined to refuse to sort on the basis of a color or form similarity. The lack of clear developmental trends here can probably be attributed to the nature of the tasks. As indicated previously, they appeared to be interesting to the children. However, if these tasks were to effectively measure children's awareness of color, as opposed to form or design, the possible choices should be varied more systematically.

Seriation Tasks. Table 8 shows the number of children who were able to complete all the seriation tasks successfully, and also those who were able to order the second set of pictures correctly after they had been given help with the first. It is interesting to compare the children's performance in these tasks with those in the conservation tasks. Where only 34 per cent of the P-1 children and 40 per cent of the P-3 children give evidence of conservation in the number tasks, 54 per cent of P-1 and 100 percent of P-3 children successfully completed at least one of the seriation problems.

Direction Tasks. These proved to be the easiest of all the tasks. Thirty-three of the P-1 children (75 per cent) spontaneously and correctly indicated the directions faced by the various figures and objects. The remainder of the children gave correct indications after inquiry on the part of the interviewers. Since the younger children did so well with these tasks, there appeared to be little point in asking the P-3 children to do them, and they were omitted in their interviews.

Summary. The ways the P-1 children responded to the various tasks posed may be described in Piagetian terms as largely "preoperational." Their thinking appears to be impressionistic and unsystematic, untroubled by logical contradiction. To a considerable extent they are beguiled by the appearance of things, interested in small details, likely to pay attention to differences about as often as to similarities, more interested in color than in form. The P-3 children are a little more systematic and somewhat less likely to focus on differences rather than similarities. As with the younger children, color appears to be a more salient property than form.

As indicated earlier, these findings can only be regarded as tentative. If one assumes for the moment that they are valid, one has to question how children who are functioning in these ways respond to arithmetic instruction. Until they shift to a more operational view of the world, can anything other than rote learning be expected?

QUESTIONS FOR FURTHER INVESTIGATION

The tentative findings also raise other questions and suggest a number of hypotheses for investigation. Which of these questions merit further research, and the conditions under which such research can most effectively be accomplished, are matters that should be decided by those responsible for educational policy in Uganda. From the viewpoint of the outsider all of them deserve some consideration.

1. To what extent are the tendencies and developmental trends suggested by these findings substantiated in a more extensive and representative sample, and with different procedures?

The need for more adequate sampling is obvious. What may be less striking, but perhaps more important, is the need for a considerable amount of experimentation with the interview procedures used to ascertain the characteristics of the children's thinking. Bearing in mind that the customary relationships between child and adult may differ from those holding in the countries where these interview procedures were developed, experimentation with different kinds of procedures seems essential. In the conservation tasks, for example, does the child in Uganda attach meanings to the orientation procedures and to the open-ended "What about now?" questions that are different from those inferred by his American counterpart? Would a more Piagetian approach, in which the child is confronted with more examples, and all of his suspect answers carefully probed, yield more valid information? Certainly such an approach ought to be tried rather extensively as a preliminary step to working out standardized procedures appropriate to children in Uganda.

Similarly, experimentation with various kinds of classification and seriation tasks seems essential. Different results may be expected depending on the objects or the pictures used, their familiarity to the children, the relative salience of their various properties, and so on.

In the present study, in most of the tasks, the objective was to capture the child's spontaneous view, to find out how he saw the world, when no specific structure was imposed on him by the adult. The assumption is that whatever the adult desires to teach has to break through the child's way of perceiving before it can be successfully incorporated into his thinking. But the fact that the child tends to focus on a particular aspect of an experience does not necessarily mean that he can not shift his attention to another aspect. Further experimentation ought to build into the tasks some measures of this kind of flexibility which is, in itself, a mark of increasing mental maturity. In the present study, for example, most of the children confronted with a blue square, a red square, and a blue circle of similar sizes would immediately choose the blue circle as being like the blue square. If the interviewer then commented that "another child" had chosen the red square, some children would insist that this was wrong because red was "not blue." But others would comment that it could be right because the red square, like the blue square, had "four corners." In the seriation tasks, some children who were initially unable to put the pictures of the women in order "from the biggest to the smallest" were able, after they had been helped to establish that correct order, to order successfully the pictures of the baskets. Other children could not.

2. To what extent does the language the children have available relate to the way they respond in the interviews? The present study assumed that the tasks posed the children were meaningful to them, and also that they had the words to express what they saw or thought. It would be appropriate, and probably revealing, to undertake a study of children's receptive and expressive vocabulary before confronting them with the kinds of tasks used here. Possible models for such studies are those of Boehm[12] and Peisach,[13] both of which deal with aspects of children's understanding of number.

3. Are the abilities involved in classification, seriation, and the understanding of space relationships developing at different rates? According to Piaget's analysis, the child's experience in classifying objects on the basis of similarities and ordering them on the basis of differences culminates in the ability to conserve number. With this progress toward operational or systematic thinking the child also becomes able to grasp such reciprocal relationships as those involved in an understanding of right and left. Replications of Piaget's work have raised questions as to whether or not development is as simultaneous in all these areas as his theory implies. The present study raises a question as to whether these children may be making more rapid progress in understanding seriation and perhaps also space relationships than they are in grasping classification and conservation. If this possibility were to be substantiated it would carry a number of implications for both curriculum and instruction.

4. How pervasive is the children's interest in color? Does it operate at the expense of an ability to deal with form? Studies of African children have sometimes carried this implication.[14] Perhaps, as suggested above, the results are, at least in part, an artifact of the methods of investigation. For children who speak Luganda, there are no words equivalent to rectangle, triangle, and so on. Are they accordingly handicapped in perceiving and conceptualizing

such forms? One wonders whether such a handicap, if it exists, applies as well to what might be termed less abstract or more natural forms, such as those encountered in leaves, flowers, fruits and so on. The cloth similarities tasks used in the present study represent one attempt at investigating this possibility. In further work the tasks will need to be modified, or new tasks designed, but it seems important to adequately ascertain the abilities of the children in this area.

5. If, as the present study suggests, conservation of number is not generally established by P-3, when is it achieved? Are there differential rates of development, depending perhaps on the home backgrounds of the children? To what extent is the ability to conserve related to success in the present mathematics program, and to success in solving various kinds of problems? To answer these questions, cross-sectional, short-term longitudinal, and experimental studies would all be in order. For example, cross-sectional studies involving children in P-1, P-3, and P-5 might be used to establish tentative norms for progress in conservation and logical thinking. Two- or three-year longitudinal studies of groups of children drawn from these same levels could provide a more adequate picture of such progress. Conceivably some groups might receive special training, or be enrolled in experimental curricula.

Without further study one would hesitate to suggest curriculum experimentation. However, it seems possible that the children would benefit from more varied experiences than they have now. Some schools use pebbles as an aid in computation, but a stable number concept probably develops from experience with the number properties of many collections of objects, variously arranged. Since experiences in classifying and ordering also contribute, more opportunities of these sorts might be incorporated into the school program. Here an essential element would appear to be the encouragement of flexibility. For example, one child might divide a collection of pebbles into groups of brown and grey. Another child might make two different groups from the same collection, based on flatness and roundness. A third might arrange the same collection in order from the smallest to the largest. Other children could "guess" the basis for each of these arrangements. Whatever experiences are provided, they ought to include opportunity for manipulation of the objects, a variety of kinds of objects, much opportunity for each child to use the appropriate language, and, to sustain interest, a gamelike orientation.

6. What are typical preschool experiences for children in Uganda? The relationships a child has had with his parents and other family members, the kinds and amounts of instruction he has had from them, the responsibilities he has learned to assume, the opportunities he has had for different kinds of play will have done much to shape his way of looking at and thinking about the world even before he enters school. There is need for systematic study of these preschool experiences and the ways they may influence later learning.

Some children begin P-1 at the age of five, some not till they are eight. The data of the present study, and some of the observations made during it, provide a hint that the children who enter later respond differently from those who enter before they are seven. Perhaps home background factors differ, or perhaps the younger ones come at the point when they are most likely to profit from instruction. On the other hand, as one of the teachers pointed out, some of the youngest may be too immature to grasp what is expected from them.

The questions that are raised here and the answers that may be found to them are, in the main, matters of general concern in the fields of developmental and educational psychology. While the questions have been posed rather specifically in terms of what is known about children and their education in Uganda, their investigation should throw light on similar questions currently being raised in other cultural settings. Research related to them may be pursued by specialists who are not identified with Uganda, provided of course that they are supported by reliable assistants and informants. But there are limitations on what the stranger can hope to accomplish. These limitations are undoubtedly of concern to those who hold responsibility for approving and supporting research in the schools of Uganda. In the case of the present study it seems clear that the validity of certain assumptions regarding the usefulness to teachers of information derived from Piagetian interviewing cannot readily, if at all, be tested by the outsider.

CONSIDERATIONS FOR THE FUTURE

The findings of the study, together with my reflections on what I saw and heard while in Uganda, suggest some considerations that may be useful in planning future research related to the early primary years.

The Stranger as Researcher. Perhaps the stranger has some advantage over his colleagues who are members of the culture in which the research is to be conducted. He has presumably a degree of objectivity and a freedom from the constraints of tradition that is lacking to them. But this advantage may be counterbalanced by his lack of knowledge of those traditions and a consequent inability to interpret what he sees and hears. Add to this, as in my own case, ignorance of the language in which his research is to be conducted, and the supposed advantages are clearly outweighed.

English is the official language in Uganda, yet one observes how often individuals who speak it fluently resort to the vernacular, usually Luganda, for amplification or perhaps clarification. To be unable to participate even in a limited way is to miss subtle but often important nuances in the ways people think and view their world. It is to be unable to communicate adequately with those who are potential contributors to the insight and understanding essential to the interpretation of the research findings.

That I was able to accomplish as much as I did, in such a short time and with as little apparent confusion, can be attributed to the patience and forbearance of my research assistants, who became increasingly open in their expression of their own bewilderment so that I could deal with it as it arose, and to the well-timed intervention of colleagues in the department of educational psychology who helped me to explain the project to school personnel.

The reactions of the assistants, who were also experienced teachers, provided some clues as to the feasibility of the teacher's use of information derived from Piagetian interviews. Other clues came from brief contacts with other teachers and from observations in the schools cooperating in the study.

The Teacher as Researcher. The matching of instruction to the ways of thinking of the child requires a teacher who has both general knowledge of what may be expected from children during a given age period or developmental stage and a repertoire of techniques to appraise the individual child. One way to acquire both knowledge and techniques is to participate in research such as the present study.

The two teachers who served as assistants are preparing for work in Teacher Training Colleges, and can probably be regarded as representative of a selected rather than typical group of Primary teachers. In a relatively short time they learned the interview procedures and, in addition to following the standardized procedure, also became skilled at asking the kinds of test questions that are essential to a more clinical approach. They reported that participation in the project made them much more alert to the interests of individual children. However, under the pressures of completing the study within a six-week period, there was almost no time for me to discuss with them the significance for instruction of whatever knowledge they may have gained.

One aspect of the study that appeared to impress both of the assistants was the distinction that had to be made between instructions or questions designed to reveal the child's way of thinking and those intended to elicit a particular response from him. It would be interesting to know to what extent an awareness of this distinction and the acquisition of some skill in diagnostic questioning may alter a teacher's perception of children's learning difficulties. For example, in the beginning of the study, one of the assistants discussing some difficulties in mathematics encountered by children in P-6 and P-7 attributed the source of difficulty to insufficient drill at earlier levels. One wonders whether his experience in interviewing younger children may lead him to speculate about the possibility that an inadequate understanding of basic concepts may be an equally or perhaps more important contributing factor.

Whether or not the teacher who has become for a time a researcher sees the relevance of his work with individual children to his work in the classroom, and indeed whether or not such research *is* truly relevant there, will depend on many factors.

The Teacher in the Classroom. The present study provided little opportunity for the researcher to become familiar with the curriculum for the early primary years—its goals, its operation, the teachers' views of it, and their preparation for it. Scanty observation of P-1 and P-3 classrooms provided only one generalization—that the similarities to early primary classrooms observed in the United States and in England were as striking as the differences. The equipment was more limited, the space more crowded; but the teachers worked with the total class, or with smaller subgroups, listened to children read, corrected the work in their copybooks, told and listened to stories, and played guessing games after the fashion of their English and American colleagues.

A considerable amount of teaching by rote, particularly in mathematics and during English instruction, was observed. On the other hand, there were teachers who varied the mathematics problems that they gave the children and who had the children use a number of different kinds of objects to solve them. There were also teachers whose English instruction was fast-moving, dependent on activity and illustration from the children, and demanding not only of chorused responses but also of answers from individual children.

To the extent that the intent of the curriculum is to develop insight and understanding on the part of the children, the techniques used in the present study, or modifications of them, do appear relevant to the classroom. Furthermore, judging from their teaching and from spontaneous comments, some of the teachers would be interested in learning such techniques and, given sufficient help, could become competent in using them.

However, what is theoretically possible may not be feasible in practice. One would hesitate to make any recommendation for the introduction of new responsibilities for already overburdened teachers, or even for teachers now being prepared, without a thorough knowledge of educational policy for Uganda and the goals it holds for both the short and long term. But whatever these may be, and despite the limitations of the present study, one prescription can be made. The teachers need to be—and to feel that they are—fully informed not only about any possible innovations, but also about any studies or research, that may be undertaken with their children or in their classrooms. While group meetings, individual conferences, and opportunities to observe the procedures to be used are time-consuming and, in the case of the researcher who is also a stranger, difficult to arrange, they are essential for the well-being of the teachers. In the present study, the teachers were cooperative and helpful, but also clearly apprehensive. Lacking sufficient information about the study when it began, they were, judging from their comments to the research assistants, never fully convinced, despite continuing reassurance, that it was not designed to evaluate them or to reflect adversely on their instruction. Whether or not their fears could have been completely allayed is uncertain, but certainly communication with them could have been more detailed and much more explicit than it was.

The apprehension of these teachers is by no means unique. Many, perhaps most, American teachers maintain a somewhat skeptical attitude toward research, based no doubt on uncertainty about its consequences for them. The reservations of teachers in Uganda, where education is so highly valued and attained at such cost, and where research is not yet extensive, are readily understood. Perhaps, however, these reservations can be overcome, with resulting benefit to education, if research can be incorporated in both pre-service and in-service teacher education. The present study has explored some of the possibilities for accomplishing this.

A PERSPECTIVE

The present study assumes that the child's learning in the first years of primary school critically influences his later learning. Considerable evidence supports this assumption. However, it has been made without reference to the specific setting of Uganda. Even if those who guide educational policy grant that the early years are crucial and deserving of intensive attention, they also confront an urgent need to provide for wider education beyond the primary school. The relative emphasis to be given early primary education and the amounts of effort and money that can go into related research are issues clearly outside the scope of this report, but their resolution bears very directly on any plans for further research.

The questions raised in the present study were formulated, and the results of the study interpreted, in the main, by an outsider with little knowledge of education in Uganda. Such a researcher brings certain kinds of knowledge and experience that may be lacking locally, but there is no guarantee that either his questions or his interpretations are as relevant as those that might be made by his colleagues who know the country better. The study would have been richer and more immediately useful, as would future studies, with a greater involvement, from the beginning, of the educators and psychologists of Uganda.

Table 1. Subjects

| | Primary-1 | | | | Primary-3 | |
| | Makerere Hill | | Kibuli | | Makere Hill | |
Age	Boys	Girls	Boys	Girls	Boys	Girls
Five	2	1	6	4		
Six	1	8	5	2		
Seven	3	1	2	1	1	
Eight	4		1	2		3
Nine			1		3	1
Ten					2	4
Eleven					4	2
Totals	10	10	15	9	10	10

Table 2. Number of children giving some evidence[a]
of conservation in each of three tasks

| | Primary-1 (N=44) | | Primary-3 (N=20) | |
Task	N	%	N	%
Counting	38	87	18	90
Number	15	34	8	40
Amount	3	7	4	20

[a] At least one indication that number or amount has not changed.

Table 3. Proportion of color responses (C) to total of color and
form responses (C+F) in four sorting tasks

| | Number of children | |
C/(C+F)	Primary-1 (N=44)	Primary-3 (N=20)
.00	13 (30%)	5 (25%)
.50	1	0
.66	3	0
.75	1	0
1.00	26 (59%)	15 (75%)

Table 4. Number of sorting tasks in which sorts were not based
on either form or color

	Number of children	
Number of Tasks	Primary-1 (*N*=44)	Primary-3 (*N*=20)
0	19 (43%)	19 (95%)
1	15	1
2	3	0
3	3	0
4	4	0

Table 5. Performance in sorting "things we can eat"
and "things we cannot eat"

	Number of children	
Performance	Primary-1 (*N*=44)	Primary-3 (*N*=20)
Correct[a]	16 (36%)	11 (55%)
3 groups[b]	14	5
Other[c]	14	4

[a] (beans) (beads and buttons)
[b] (beans) (beads) (buttons)
[c] no sorting or designs

Table 6. Proportion of color responses (C) to total of color and form
responses (C+F) in 9 cloth similarities tasks

	Number of children	
C/(C+F)	Primary-1 (*N* = 44)	Primary-3 (*N* = 20)
0–.25	3	0
.26–.50	2	1
.51–.75	18	6
.76–1.00	21	13

Table 7. Number of times neither form nor color was chosen in 9
cloth similarities tasks

	Number of children	
Number of Times	Primary-1 (N = 44)	Primary-3 (N = 20)
0	17	8
1	3	6
2	6	1
3	6	0
4	9	1
5	2	4
6	0	0
7	0	0
8	0	0
9	1	0

Table 8. Performance in seriation tasks

	Number of children	
	Primary-1 (N = 44)	Primary-3 (N = 20)
All correct	17	18
One correct	7	2
Other	20	0

II
Two Reports of Research in Child Growth and Development

JOEL R. DAVITZ

This report reviews the results of two exploratory studies of school children in Uganda,[1] the first dealing with emotional experiences and the second with productive thinking. A final section presents some general comments based on impressions gained during the course of the project.

REPORTED EMOTIONAL EXPERIENCES OF UGANDAN CHILDREN

The first study to be considered involves children's descriptions of emotional experiences. The aims of this research were to describe systematically the emotional experiences reported by children, to explore possible differences in these reports as a function of sex of the child and the language used, and to develop more specific problems for further research along this line of investigation.

Method

The subjects of this research were 107 students between the ages of twelve and twenty enrolled at Makerere Hill Primary School and Naguru/Katali Primary School in Kampala, Uganda. Of the 107 children, 30 either failed to complete the task or did not follow instructions in writing their reports. In order to equate sample size for the subgroups treated in the subsequent analysis, 15 subjects in each of the following four groups were randomly selected: (1) Boys who wrote in English; (2) Boys who wrote in Luganda; (3) Girls who wrote in English; (4) Girls who wrote in Luganda. Thus the final analysis of the data was based on a sample of 60 children, which provided a basis for comparing the experiences of boys and girls and the reports written in English and Luganda.

The 107 subjects were seen in class groups, each session lasting about one hour. They were given their choice of responding in Luganda or in English; 34 chose to write in Luganda and 73 in English. The purpose and procedures of the study were first explained to the children orally, and they were encouraged to ask as many questions as they liked to clarify the instructions. The report forms were handed out, and once again the instructions were given and questions answered. Then, each child was asked to describe three emotional experiences, in the following order: happiness, sadness, and anger. A critical-incident technique was used: the child was first asked to think of a particular time he had been happy, and then to describe as fully as he could the experience of happiness. The children were given fifteen minutes to write their descriptions. The same instructions were then repeated for the experience of sadness and finally for the experience of anger.

Analysis of Data

The data were treated by means of a content analysis. On the basis of previous research and a preliminary review of the present data, categories of analysis were developed and are presented in outline form below. The first three major categories concern level of activation; the next three deal with relatedness to the environment, labeled in terms of moving toward, away from, or against others. Two categories involve aspects of adequacy and functioning, one in terms of inadequacy or dysfunctioning and the other of self-enhancement. The next two categories refer to feelings of discomfort and comfort, and the remaining categories focus on attitudes, expressive behavior, self-awareness, hunger, a sense of unreality, and other feelings elicited during the experience. Finally, the situations mentioned in the reports were broadly categorized, producing a separate set of situation categories for each of the three different emotions.

Content Categories

HYPOACTIVATION
    Including weakness, tiredness, heaviness, emptiness.

ACTIVATION
    Including energetic, excited, physical expressions of activation.

HYPERACTIVATION
    Including physical manifestations such as heart pounding, bursting.

MOVE TOWARD OTHERS
    1. General—want want to be with, help, talk to others.
    2. Absence of negative feelings toward others.

MOVE AWAY FROM OTHERS
1. Escape situation, not talk to others, be alone.
2. Wish to die.

MOVE AGAINST OTHERS
1. Impulse to extreme aggression (usually involving death of other)—not acted out.
2. Impulse to aggression—not acted out.
3. Aggressive behavior (interpersonal)—acted out.
4. Aggressive behavior (objects or general)—acted out.
5. Nonphysical aggression (verbal, resistance)—acted out.
6. Aggression toward self (including self-derogation).
7. Control of aggression (including both internal and external control).

INADEQUACY, HELPLESSNESS
1. General sense of inadequacy.
2. General dysfunction.
3. Speech dysfunction.
4. Sensory dysfunction.
5. Cognitive dysfunction; obsessive thoughts.
6. Motor dysfunction; random activity.

SELF-ENHANCEMENT
1. General—including ability, position.
2. Strength.

DISCOMFORT
1. General—sickness, pains.
2. Heat, fever.
3. Cold.
4. Tension.

COMFORT
1. General.
2. Freedom from worry, pain, death, negative feelings.

ATTITUDE (General view of world, future).
1. Positive.
2. Negative.

EXPRESSIVE BEHAVIOR
1. Laughing, smiling, singing.
2. Crying.

28

SELF-AWARENESS
  1. Self-absorbed.
  2. Lack or loss of self-awareness, self-motivation.

HUNGER
  1. Absence hunger.
  2. Not eat.

SENSE OF UNREALITY

OTHER FEELINGS ELICITED
  1. Anxiety, fear.
  2. Guilt.
  3. Sadness, depression.

Situation Categories

ANGER
  1. Aggression by adult.
  2. Aggression by child.
  3. Other.
  4. Not specified.

SADNESS
  1. Death.
  2. Academic failure.
  3. Other.
  4. Not specified.

HAPPINESS
  1. Academic success.
  2. Visit relatives, friends.
  3. Social affair.
  4. Presents, gifts, surprises.
  5. Other.
  6. Not specified.

Results

The data obtained for each emotional state—happiness, sadness, and anger—will be summarized in tabular form and briefly discussed. The analysis, in terms of numbers of children who mentioned the various categories, allows comparison of the reports of the four subgroups, of the reports written by boys with those written by girls, and of the reports written in English with those written in Luganda. Discussion focuses on the quality and predominant characteristics of the children's descriptions, as indicated by the relative frequencies with which the categories and situations were mentioned by the group as a whole.

Happiness. Table 1 summarizes the content of the descriptions of happiness. The first comparison is in terms of the number of subjects in each subgroup who mentioned a particular category. Thus, for example, 7 of the 15 boys who wrote their descriptions in English mentioned activation in their reports, and 6 of the 15 subjects in each of the other three subgroups mentioned activation.

For an over-all view of the results, reference may be made to the totals column, paying particular attention to those categories with relatively high frequencies. Happiness was characterized most frequently by references to expressive behavior such as laughing and smiling, and to a sense of activation, frequently expressed by energetic activity. Also mentioned with relatively high frequency was freedom from negative feelings such as worry, pain, and concern about death. In addition, the children often mentioned various aspects of self-enhancement through special status. Finally, among the relatively high-frequency categories was the impulse to move toward other people, especially friends and relatives typically mentioned in the context of sharing the child's own experience of happiness.

The situations associated with happiness most often involved academic success, with much lower frequencies in all the other situation categories.

There appear to be no considerable differences between the reports written in English and those written in Luganda, or between the descriptions given by boys and those given by girls. Boys somewhat more frequently mention freedom from worry, etc., and academic success; but these differences are small and may well be chance findings.

Sadness. Descriptions of the children's experience of sadness were particularly rich in detail and dramatically presented. The data are summarized in Table 2.

Crying and other intense expressions of grief, such as throwing oneself on the ground and beating one's head, were most frequently mentioned, almost always associated with the death of a parent, sibling, or other relative—death being by far the most frequent occasion of sadness. In addition, sadness was typically characterized by a wish to be alone, to withdraw from others, sometimes expressed in a most extreme form as a wish to escape by dying. Also commonly associated with death were obsessive thoughts recalling past experiences with, or problems of living without, the love and support of a deceased parent, sibling, aunt, uncle, or grandparent. Finally, sadness was often characterized by inability to eat, by a totally pessimistic view of the world and particularly of the future, and by general physical discomfort.

All in all, the children described sadness as an extraordinarily painful, traumatic experience; and many of their reports suggested that even long after the event, the experience is vividly remembered.

Differences between the reports of boys and girls, or between those written in English and Luganda, appear to be negligible.

Anger. Among these children, according to their reports, anger is occasioned most frequently by an attack, either by an adult or another child. When the attack is by an adult, the most typical response is withdrawal or escape from the situation and expressive behavior such as crying. (Table 3.)

As might be expected, anger is also accompanied by aggressive impulses; but the particular pattern of these impulses is worth noting. Most frequent is an impulse to extreme aggression, typically involving the death and destruction of another person. Nearly as frequent is inclination to moderate aggression, such as striking or kicking the other person. The moderately aggressive impulses are sometimes acted out, but never in relation to an adult. Thus, when attacked or punished by an adult, the child is likely to experience some impulse to aggression, frequently in an extreme form, but the impulse is inhibited and the child attempts to escape from the situation. If the other person in the situation is a child, some moderate aggression may be actually expressed, either verbally or physically.

Finally, anger is also accompanied among these children by various kinds of physical discomfort, a sense of enhanced strength, and feelings of hyperactivation.

Certain differences may be noted between boys' and girls' descriptions of anger, particularly in relation to aggressive impulses. Boys more frequently reported impulses to extreme aggression and a sense of greatly enhanced strength, while girls more frequently said they resorted to verbal and other nonphysical forms of aggression.

The reports written in English mentioned impulses to extreme aggression more often than the Luganda reports did. However, this is the only substantial difference among all the categories and is likely to be a chance finding.

Discussion

Perhaps the most striking feature of this research is the extraordinary emotional sensitivity revealed by the children's reports. With relatively few exceptions, the children were capable of writing remarkably rich, vivid, and complex descriptions of their emotional experiences, reflecting a very high degree of sensitivity and self-awareness. It would probably not be profitable at this point to speculate much about cultural determinants of this sensitivity; further descriptive work must be done with larger and perhaps more representative samples of Ugandan children before embarking on research designed to discover the specific antecedents of this apparently high degree of sensitivity. Nevertheless, in terms of understanding the development of Ugandan children as well as gaining knowledge relevant to other cultures, the results of the present study underscore the potential significance of further research along this line of investigation. For example, if particular child-rearing variables characteristic of the Ugandan culture could be identified as specific antecedents of subsequent emotional sensitivity, such research would have obvious theoretical significance as well as broad implications for child-rearing in other cultures.

From the perspective of a researcher coming to Uganda from another culture, one of the most dramatic observations of this research is the disparity between the children's typically nonexpressive behavior in interaction with adults in school settings and the intense emotional experiences described in their written reports. On the basis of their everyday interactions with adults in the relatively formal situation of the school, an adult unfamiliar with the backgrounds of these children might infer that they have limited and superficial emotional reactions. Because they tend to be overtly impassive and emotionally unexpressive in relating to adults in school settings, one might conclude that their inner emotional life also tends to be flat and restricted. But in fact, if the results of this research are at all valid, just the opposite seems to be the case. Despite their apparent overt impassivity in certain formal situations, most of the children have extremely strong and varied emotional reactions.

For an observer intimately familiar with the Ugandan culture, this observation is not likely to seem particularly striking or remarkable. The disparity between overt behavior and inner emotional experience is perhaps accepted and understood as a norm of the culture. Nevertheless, even for those adults who are intellectually aware of this discrepancy, as a consequence of day-to-day contact with children who tend to be relatively unexpressive, it is possible to slip without awareness into the false assumption that these children experience constricted emotional reactions. And it takes little imagination indeed to picture the unfortunate consequences of such a misunderstanding in a teacher-student relationship. There is no sure antidote for this kind of difficulty, and it may not be a significant or common problem in the schools. However, as a technique designed to reinforce an adult's understanding of the children with whom he is working, the simple procedures for the collection of data in this study might occasionally be useful to teachers in the schools. This does not mean that the teacher should engage in the more formal analysis of data reported in this study; but reading such reports would probably give teachers more insight into the depth and intensity of their pupils' emotional experiences.

Of the three emotional states considered in this research, sadness was described with the greatest dramatic detail, suggesting the hypothesis that sadness is experienced by these children with special intensity. Death is by far the most commonly reported occasion for sadness, and this finding suggests a possible interpretation of the apparent intensity of these experiences. First, within a large extended family the death of a family member is a relatively frequent event; and in the family structure characteristic of Uganda (as contrasted with that of cultures in which distant relatives may have little or nothing to do with each other), the death of even a distant relative is likely to have personal meaning for the child. Moreover, the intense expressions of grief characteristically associated with death in Uganda may serve to reinforce the strength of a child's personal reactions. And finally, of course, quite apart from the emotional trauma, the death of a parent may often have severe practical consequences that radically change a child's life. Thus, as a function of certain cultural factors, the death of a relation and the associated emotional reactions of sadness are likely to be experienced with particular intensity. These speculations obviously need to be investigated in much more detail, and further research might profitably focus on reactions to death and the experience of sadness within the various subcultures of Uganda.

A number of reports written by the children in the present sample suggest that their feelings of sadness continue for rather extended periods after the precipitating event. For example, children report that even long after the death of a parent or grandparent, they become miserably unhappy and in a sense "relive" the experience of sadness whenever they recall the event. This might conceivably reflect some degree of unresolved grief among these children, perhaps engendered by the extreme intensity of their initial emotional reactions, and further research might investigate this phenomenon in terms of the subsequent psychological adjustment of these children.

The data also suggest a potentially fruitful line of investigation in regard to the experience of anger. Anger in relation to adults would seem to present a particularly complex and significant problem. Many of these children report having extremely violent aggressive impulses when angered by an adult; but these impulses are rarely if ever expressed in any direct fashion. They are almost always inhibited, the usual reaction involving withdrawal or escape from the immediate situation, with continued unresolved anger. The present research provided no evidence about the consequences of these experiences, in terms of psychological impact; but the combination of strong aggressive impulses and rigorous inhibition of any expression of these impulses in relation to adults suggests a number of hypotheses. For example, one might expect to find among school children a fairly high incidence of malaise or even depression, perhaps some psychosomatic manifestations, probably a good deal of displaced aggression toward each other or toward younger children, and perhaps occasional violent and apparently irrational outbursts directed at authority figures in the schools. These speculations, of course, merely suggest hypotheses that might be tested in further research.

Another point suggested by the data concerns the provocation of anger. In most instances the provocation involves an attack by another person, but when the attack is made by an adult, the children seem to react not so much to the attack *per se* as to the apparent unreasonableness or injustice of the adult's aggression. In other words, it is not the pain or punishment itself that angers and disturbs the child, but the unanswerable unfairness of the adult. Once again, this can only provide a potentially interesting lead for further research, but it suggests at least that in disciplining these children in the schools, the rational basis for any punishment must be made abundantly clear to the child. Otherwise, he is likely to perceive the punishment as another instance of adult injustice against which he is powerless to act, thus adding to his store of unresolved anger directed at the adult world.

In regard to the children's descriptions of happiness, perhaps the most obvious point to note is that the occasions for happiness most often cited by these children involved some kind of academic success—usually the passing of a major examination. Probably no one concerned with education in Uganda needs any research to tell him about the importance of academic success for most of the children in the schools. But in any event, the results of this study underscore this rather obvious point. Note that the children were asked to think of *any* happy experience they had ever had. It is true, of course, that the data were collected in schools, and this undoubtedly biased the results somewhat. Nevertheless, it still seems remarkable that the one type of occasion associated with happiness by any large proportion of children involved academic success. Although this may well be an obvious finding for most educators in Uganda, it reaffirms the overwhelming significance of school experiences in the emotional lives of Ugandan children.

PRODUCTIVE THINKING AMONG UGANDAN CHILDREN

The purpose of this study was to investigate productive thinking among Ugandan children in relation to age, sex, and the language used by the child in reporting his responses. In addition, from a methodological point of view, a primary aim of the study was to evaluate a technique of measurement in terms of its usefulness for further research and for the development of measures relevant to the evaluation of intellectual abilities.

Method

The subjects of this research were 30 children enrolled at Naguru/Katali Primary School in Kampala, Uganda. The total sample was divided into six subgroups of 5 children each, on the basis of age, sex, and language used in administration of the procedures and reporting of responses. These subgroups were as follows: (1) Older boys who reported in English; (2) Older boys who reported in Luganda; (3) Older girls who reported in English; (4) Older girls who reported in Luganda; (5) Younger boys who reported in Luganda; (6) Younger girls who reported in Luganda. A summary of descriptive information about the sample is presented in Table 4.

The procedure used to collect data involved a modification of a technique developed by Wallach and Kogan and described in *Modes of Thinking in Young Children* (1965).[2] The interview schedule consists of five sections: (1) Instances of general categories; (2) Alternate uses of common objects; (3) Similarities between objects; (4) Meanings of graphic patterns; (5) Meanings of line drawings. The interview schedule as adapted is shown on pages 34–37.

The entire procedure was presented to the child as a game, emphasizing throughout that there were no specific right answers to any question, and that we were interested in any idea that occurred to the child. The child was encouraged to take as long a time as he wanted for each item, and the length of time required for the interviews varied from one to three hours. All responses were tape-recorded and the scores based on transcriptions of these recordings.

INSTRUCTIONS FOR ADMINISTERING
WALLACH–KOGAN CREATIVITY QUESTIONNAIRE

I. *Instances*

"In this game I am going to tell you something and it will be your job to name as many things as you can think of that are like what I tell you. For example, I might say 'things that taste good.' (The experimenter then lets the child try.) "Yes, those are fine. Some other kinds of things might be sweets, cake, or sugar." (Here the experimenter varies his suggestions so that they consist of ones which the child has not provided.) "So we see that there are all kinds of different answers in this game. Do you see how we play?" (If the child already indicated strong understanding, the last sentence is replaced by, "I can see you already know how we play this game.") "Now remember, I will name something and you are supposed to name as many things as you can think of that are like what I've said. All right, let's go."

1. Name all the round things you can think of.

2. Name all the things you can think of that will make a noise.

3. Name all the things you can think of that move on wheels.

II. *Alternate Uses*

"Now, in this game, I am going to name an object—any kind of object, like a piece of wood or a ball—and it will be your job to tell me lots of different ways that the object can be used. Any object can be used in a lot of different ways. For example, think about string. What are some of the ways you can think of that you might use string?" (The experimenter lets the child try.) "Yes, those are fine. I was thinking that you could also use string to attach a fish hook, to sew with, to hang clothes on." (The experimenter varies his suggestions so as not to duplicate any the child has provided.) "There are lots more, too, and yours were very good examples. I can see that you already understand how we play this game. So let's begin now. And remember, think of all the different ways you could use the object I name. Here we go."

1. Tell me all the different ways you could use a banana leaf.

2. Tell me all the different ways you could use a knife.

3. Tell me all the different ways you could use a tin.

4. Tell me all the different ways you could use a table.

III. *Similarities*

"In this game I am going to name two things, and I will want you to think of all the ways these two things are alike. I might say any two things—like door and chair. But whatever I say, it will be your job to think of all the ways that the two things are alike. (For example, tell me all the ways that an orange and a mango are alike." (The child then responds.) "That's very good. You've already said a lot of things I was thinking of. I guess you could also say that they are both sweet, they both have seeds, they both are fruits, they both have skins, they both grow on trees—things like that. Yours were fine, too." (The experimenter's suggestions are varied so as not to include any which the child has given.) "Do you see how to play the game?" (or, "I can see that you already know how to play this game.") "Well, let's begin now. And remember, each time I name two things, you name as many ways as you can that these two things are alike."

1. Tell me all the ways in which a potato and a cassava are alike.

2. Tell me all the ways in which a cat and a mouse are alike.

3. Tell me all the ways in which a bicycle and a motorcycle are alike.

4. Tell me all the ways in which milk and meat are alike.

5. Tell me all the ways in which a shop and a market are alike.

IV. Pattern Meanings

"Here's a game where you can really feel free to use your imagination. In this game I am going to show you some drawings. After looking at each one, I want you to tell me all the things you think each drawing could be. Here is an example—you can turn it anyway you like." (The experimenter gives the example card to the child.) "What could this be?" (The child is encouraged to try some suggestions.) "Yes, those are fine. Some other kinds of things I was thinking of were the rising sun, eye lashes, a brush, and probably there are lots of other things, too. And yours were very good examples, too." (The experimenter's particular suggestions are varied so as not to include any given by the child.) "I can see that you already know how we play this game. So, let's begin now."

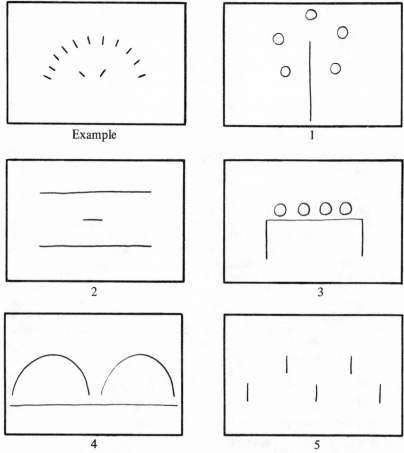

FIGURE 1. Stimulus materials for the Pattern Meanings procedure. (Original cards, 4 in. × 6 in.)

V. *Line Meanings*

"This game is called the line game. I am going to show you some lines and after you have looked at each one, I want you to tell me all the things it makes you think of. Now take your time, and be sure that when you look at the line you tell me what the whole line makes you think of, and not just a part of it. All right?"

The experimenter then presents the first of the five items in this procedure. Each line is shown on a separate card (4″ X 6″).

"Here is the first line. You can turn it any way you want to. Tell me all the things you can about it. What does it make you think of?"

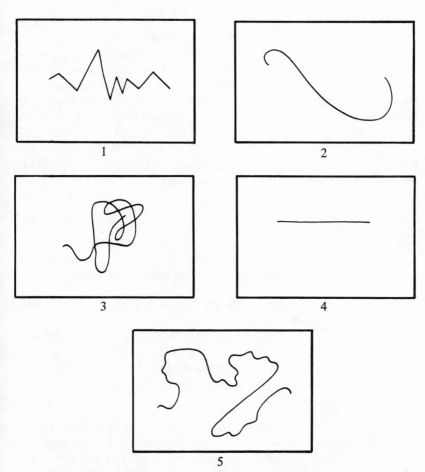

FIGURE 2. Stimulus materials for the Line Meanings procedure. (Original cards, 4 in. X 6 in.)

Wallach and Kogan developed this instrument as a measure of creative thinking, based on an associative model of creativity. Essentially, they suggested that creative thinking could reasonably be defined operationally in terms of the number of ideas generated about a particular problem and the novelty or uniqueness of these ideas. Subsequent research by these investigators has demonstrated that while the five sections of the interview schedule are positively intercorrelated, performance on these tasks is independent of usual measures of intelligence.

Items were modified in order to make them appropriate for children in Uganda. Thus, for example, in asking for alternate uses of common objects, items such as banana leaf, knife, and tin were chosen. In each case, care was taken to assure that the child was in fact familiar with the objects mentioned in each section.

For purposes of the present analysis, only the number of ideas generated by each child was considered. Obtaining an adequate measure of uniqueness depends upon normative data from a much larger sample than could possibly be tested in the present study. Therefore, rather than interpret the results in terms of creativity, it seems more reasonable to consider the present data as measures of capacity for productive thinking—assuming that productivity as defined operationally by the quantity of ideas generated is an important aspect of creativity. Perhaps more important than a concern about whether or not this measure provides a valid estimate of creativity is the fact that the tasks offer an opportunity for studying aspects of children's thinking which appear to be independent of more commonly used tests of intelligence.

Results

The over-all results for each subgroup are summarized in Table 5. Because of the nature of the distribution, the median and range for each subtest for each group are presented rather than means and standard deviations.

Differences among Subtests. The children seemed generally to be most productive in giving instances of general categories and alternate uses of common objects. In contrast, they seem to have been least productive in responding to graphic stimuli, both for patterns and line meanings. In general, performance on the similarities subtest was between the two extremes, not as productive as in giving either instances or alternate uses, but more productive than in dealing with graphic stimuli.

Difference between Languages. It is interesting to note that all the interviewers involved in the collection of these data were convinced that those children who responded in English were much less productive than those who responded in Luganda. However, the data do not support this conclusion consistently, and it seems likely that the judgment was based on the children's apparent difficulties with vocal expression in English rather than on the quantity of productivity itself. Although no systematic record of time required for each interview was kept, it seemed to the interviewers that the interviews in English generally took much longer than those in Luganda, and that some children responding in English experienced considerably more difficulty and expended much greater effort than those responding in Luganda. On some occasions it seemed as if the child had to translate the question from English into Luganda and then translate the answer from Luganda into English. These, of course, are speculative inferences, but the informal observations on which they are based do suggest that some of the children had considerable difficulty with the mechanics of vocal communication in English.

Nevertheless, a number of the children were remarkably productive in English. In particular, the older boys responding in English seem to have done as well as, or better than, those responding in Luganda. The older girls responding in Luganda were generally more productive on the verbal items, while those responding in English were slightly more productive on the graphic tasks.

Thus, despite whatever difficulties the children may have had in vocal expression, there was no consistent pattern of greater productivity in one language or the other for the total group of older boys and girls. Inspection of Table 6, however, suggests that while median values are not consistently different, the range of scores is considerably greater in English than in Luganda for four of the five subtests. Therefore, children's performances on cognitive tasks such as those used in the present research may well be much more variable in English than in Luganda simply as a consequence of individual differences in their knowledge of English rather than in their intellectual capacity for productive thinking.

Sex and Age Differences. As indicated in Table 5, among the older subjects who responded in English and the younger subjects who responded in Luganda, boys were clearly more productive than girls. However, this sex difference did not hold among the older children who responded in Luganda. The data at least suggest the existence of some interaction effect between language and age; but the group sample size is very small, and it is obvious that further research is needed to clarify this interaction.

Finally, controlling for language by comparing results only for those groups who responded in Luganda, the results summarized in Table 6 suggest that the older students were somewhat more productive on the verbal tasks but not on the two graphic subtests.

Discussion

Although the results of this study must be treated with caution, primarily because of the small sample size of each group, the data suggest a number of possible leads for further research and some implications both for teaching and for test development.

Comparison of performances on the several subtests revealed greatest productivity in generating ideas about instances of general categories and alternate uses of common objects. In fact, a number of the children showed an astonishing ability to produce ideas in these areas, often with considerable ingenuity and flexibility. In teaching, therefore, it would seem reasonable to take advantage of these cognitive strengths and perhaps develop specific teaching techniques based on this kind of ability. For example, in developing any generalization in a given subject area, such as the concept of set in mathematics, the teacher might well rely on the pupils' abilities to identify specific instances of a general category, gradually shaping the concept by selective reinforcement of pupil responses. Thus, concept development may proceed most effectively by starting with an approximation of the generalization desired, eliciting specific instances of the general category, and selectively reinforcing these responses. The present study, of course, does not directly support this hypothesis, but the data lend credence to the notion that teaching techniques based on the abilities of the children to enumerate specific instances of a general category may be particularly effective.

The children in this sample were least able to respond productively to the graphic stimuli. On the basis of so few children, and with the limited sample of behavior obtained in this study, it would be unreasonable to make any firm generalizations about Ugandan children's ability to deal with graphic stimuli. The data, however, at least suggest further exploration along this line, perhaps investigating cognitive responses to a variety of stimuli presented in different modes. If further research should indeed support the tentative findings of this study, then certainly important steps in educational practice would be implied. Perhaps a wider range of experiences and a greater frequency of exposure to graphically presented symbols, with appropriate cognitive exercises, might profitably be built into the curriculum, thus strengthening these cognitive abilities among the students.

Undoubtedly, the most important finding in regard to differences in productivity as a function of language is the wide range of performance found among those who responded in English. Assuming the data validly reflect individual differences in the ability to use English, the results indicate that children with tremendously divergent abilities in English are often in the same class. In the present sample, the children from the same class ranged from those who were barely able to produce one or two responses to most of the questions to those who displayed truly remarkable productive capacities.

In view of the fact that these differences were especially striking among the groups who responded in English, with much smaller ranges found among those who responded in Luganda, it is most reasonable to account for this observation in terms of ability to use English rather than in terms of cognitive capacity to perform the tasks *per se*. In either case, if teaching in English, the teacher is likely to encounter an extremely wide range of abilities among students in any given class. This, of course, presents special problems of instruction which may seriously interfere with the learning of individual students, and it would therefore seem to be of primary importance for further research to investigate teaching and learning problems as a function of wide individual differences among pupils.

Early in the course of this research it became apparent that a number of children had considerable difficulty in understanding and following the instructions for each subtest. Therefore, a good deal of care was taken to assure that each child understood the nature of the task; this sometimes required that the instructions be repeated, reworded, and illustrated many times. Otherwise, much of the variance in the results might have been accounted for by whether or not a child understood the requirements of each task.

This observation implies certain methodological safeguards for future research, with frequent checks built into any research procedure to make sure that instructions are fully understood. But of more immediate importance is the implication of this observation for the development of a testing program in the schools. Unless a test is designed specifically to measure a child's ability to follow instructions, every effort should be made to keep instructions as simple as possible and to provide adequate checks on the child's understanding of what he is required to do. Without this precaution, as new forms of testing are introduced in the schools, the test results might well be in large part a function of the instructions used rather than of the knowledge or ability presumably being measured. Similarly, in teaching, to minimize misunderstanding whenever new learning material or a new procedure is introduced, the teacher might well devote a substantial period of his initial instruction to clarification of the tasks involved.

This problem is complicated by these children's tendency to "go along" with whatever an adult says. Thus, when asked if he understands a given task, a child might say yes even though his understanding of the task is in fact quite limited. If this is a general phenomenon, it seems likely that learning as well as test performance might be seriously impaired. Therefore, whenever possible, it would seem desirable for teachers to encourage pupils to express their lack of understanding and to question adults when they need further clarification.

From a broader perspective, this research has some implications for the development of a testing program in the schools. By and large, most standardized tests of intellectual ability comprise questions that have single correct answers, and a child's ability is evaluated on the basis of whether or not he knows these particular answers. This is without doubt an important kind of intellectual ability, and tests of this sort have proven useful in other countries.

But it would be unfortunate if test development in Uganda were to be limited to this aspect of cognitive activity. Particularly in a rapidly developing country, where new challenges and new problems are encountered frequently, there should be a premium on productive, creative thinking that generates new ideas and new solutions. For many of the problems the child will encounter in subsequent schooling and certainly outside of school, ready-made solutions simply are not available, and his success will often depend largely on his ability to generate new ideas. This is precisely the kind of cognitive task involved in the procedures of this research, and while other specific procedures may prove to be more useful, it would seem wise to incorporate this kind of cognitive performance in any program of test development.

SOME GENERAL COMMENTS

Throughout this report, a number of specific findings and suggestions for further research have been discussed. At this point I should like to indulge in a few general comments about my experiences during the project.

One of the most impressive aspects of this experience was the interest in psychological and educational research expressed by almost everyone I met during the course of my work. Of course my contacts were selective, and one might reasonably expect a receptivity to research activities among those with whom I worked. I have gathered from comments made by others that this current interest in research reflects a relatively recent development in attitudes; however that may be, this actively positive view of research seems to be widespread among those I have met who are involved in education.

Thus, the current situation in Uganda appears to be highly favorable for initiating a more vigorous program of educational research. Moreover, a multitude of problems await investigation that would have both general theoretical interest as well as more immediate, practical implications. Even though my stay in Uganda was relatively short, I soon became aware of a variety of challenging and researchable problems that demand systematic investigation. In fact, it would be unfortunate to regard educational research in Uganda as a luxury. In a rapidly developing and changing country, extremely complex and significant problems are encountered with almost every major decision, and it seems unlikely that these problems can be resolved adequately on the basis of knowledge and experience gained in other cultural settings. If these decisions are to be made effectively, they must be based on systematic knowledge—and this, of course, implies a rigorous research basis for educational practice.

Assuming that the need and opportunity for educational research are obvious, a number of possible models might be followed. The present project provides one possibility, relying on visiting researchers who pursue short-term, specific, and limited investigations. As an initial stage in developing a research program, this has certain values both for the visitors and for those involved in education in Uganda. But in the long run, this pattern of research activity has serious limitations. Significant, meaningful questions for research are much more likely to be formulated by those who have direct experience with educational problems in Uganda over an extended period of time. In addition, single studies of particular problems are unlikely to provide the systematic, cumulative knowledge necessary for effective and rational decision-making.

Therefore, an on-going, long-term, coordinated program of research seems most desirable, probably devoted largely to the major practical and immediate problems of education in Uganda, but also gradually accumulating a store of knowledge that will have broader and more general value. Such a program, of course, would have to be implemented with a coordinated program of training in educational research, designed to prepare professional personnel who would subsequently devote their careers to problems of educational research in Uganda. Thus, both research and training would represent supplementary aspects of an over-all program in education.

Table 1. Number of Subjects Who Mentioned Each Category in Their Descriptions of Happiness

Category	Totals	Comparison by Subgroup				Comparison by Sex		Comparison by Language	
		Boys in English	Boys in Luganda	Girls in English	Girls in Luganda	Boys	Girls	English	Luganda
Activation	25	7	6	6	6	13	12	13	12
Hyperactivation	7	2	3	1	1	5	2	3	4
Move toward others	14	4	2	4	4	6	8	8	6
Absence of negative feelings toward others	5	3	—	2	—	3	2	5	—
General dysfunctioning	4	—	—	2	2	—	4	2	2
Speech dysfunctioning	3	—	1	2	—	1	2	2	1
Sensory dysfunctioning	2	—	2	—	—	2	—	—	2
Cognitive dysfunctioning	5	1	1	3	—	2	3	4	1
Motor dysfunctioning	2	—	1	1	—	1	1	1	1
Enhancement, general	18	5	4	5	4	9	9	10	8
Enhanced strength	2	—	2	—	—	2	—	—	2
Discomfort, general	1	—	1	—	—	1	—	—	1
Heat, fever	4	1	3	—	—	4	—	1	3
Comfort, general	12	3	4	2	3	7	5	5	7
Freedom from worry, pain, death, etc.	21	7	6	5	3	13	8	12	9
Positive attitude toward world, future	9	3	3	2	1	6	3	5	4

Expressive behavior: Smile, laugh, etc.	27	8	7	9	3	15	12	17	10
Expressive behavior: Crying	10	4	3	2	1	7	3	6	4
Self-absorbed	7	1	2	3	1	3	4	4	3
Loss of self-awareness	3	—	2	—	1	2	1	—	3
Absence of hunger	3	—	2	—	1	2	1	—	3
Not eat	4	1	—	2	1	1	3	3	1
Sense of unreality	7	1	3	2	1	4	3	3	4
Other feelings: Anxiety, fear	1	—	1	—	—	1	—	—	1
SITUATIONS									
Academic success	20	6	6	4	4	12	8	10	10
Visit parents, relatives, friends	9	2	2	3	2	4	5	5	4
Social affair	4	1	1	1	1	2	2	2	2
Receive presents	9	2	—	3	4	2	7	5	4
Other	7	2	3	—	2	5	2	2	5
Not specified	11	2	3	4	2	5	6	6	5

Table 2. Number of Subjects Who Mentioned Each Category in Their Descriptions of Sadness

Category	Totals	Comparison by Subgroup				Comparison by Sex		Comparison by Language	
		Boys in English	Boys in Luganda	Girls in English	Girls in Luganda	Boys	Girls	English	Luganda
Hypoactivation	18	6	4	4	4	10	8	10	8
Move away from others	21	7	3	8	3	10	11	15	6
Wish to die	12	3	2	5	2	5	7	8	4
Impulse to extreme aggression	1	–	1	–	–	1	–	–	1
Impulse to moderate aggression	1	–	–	1	–	–	1	1	–
Aggression toward self	5	3	–	–	2	3	2	3	2
General sense of inadequacy	2	–	1	1	–	1	1	1	1
General dysfunction	7	–	3	3	1	3	4	3	4
Speech dysfunction	3	1	1	–	1	2	1	1	2
Sensory dysfunction	2	1	1	–	–	2	–	1	1
Cognitive dysfunction	11	2	5	3	1	7	4	5	6
Obsessive thoughts	19	3	3	6	7	6	13	9	10
Motor dysfunction	4	1	1	2	–	2	2	3	1
Random activity	2	1	–	–	1	1	1	1	1

General discomfort	13	3	4	4	2	7	6	7	6
Heat, fever	5	2	2	1	–	4	1	3	2
Cold	1	1	–	–	–	1	–	1	–
Tension	2	1	1	–	–	2	–	1	1
Negative attitude toward world, future	15	3	3	5	4	6	9	8	7
Expressive behavior: Crying	33	8	7	10	8	15	18	18	15
Loss of self-awareness	3	–	2	1	–	2	1	1	2
Not eat	18	3	3	6	6	6	12	9	9
Sense of unreality	2	–	1	1	–	1	1	1	1
Other feelings:									
Anxiety, fear	1	–	1	–	–	1	–	–	1
Guilt	3	1	2	–	–	3	–	1	2
SITUATIONS									
Death	34	8	10	8	8	18	16	16	18
Academic failure	5	2	–	1	2	2	3	3	2
Other	12	3	3	1	5	6	6	4	8
Not specified	9	2	2	5	–	4	5	7	2

Table 3. Number of Subjects Who Mentioned Each Category in Their Descriptions of Anger

Category	Totals	Comparison by Subgroup				Comparison by Sex		Comparison by Language	
		Boys in English	Boys in Luganda	Girls in English	Girls in Luganda	Boys	Girls	English	Luganda
Hypoactivation	2	1	–	–	1	1	1	1	1
Activation	3	–	1	2	–	1	2	2	1
Hyperactivation	8	4	1	2	1	5	3	6	2
Move away from others	22	6	4	6	6	10	12	12	10
Wish to die	5	1	–	–	4	1	4	1	4
Impulse to extreme aggression (not acted out)	18	8	5	4	1	13	5	12	6
Impulse to moderate aggression (not acted out)	17	4	4	6	3	8	9	10	7
Aggressive behavior (toward persons)	11	4	–	3	4	4	7	7	4
Aggressive behavior (toward objects)	6	–	2	2	2	2	4	2	4
Nonphysical aggression (e.g. verbal)	10	1	1	5	3	2	8	6	4
Aggression toward self	2	–	1	–	1	1	1	–	2
Control of aggression	4	3	–	1	–	3	1	4	–
General sense of inadequacy	2	1	–	–	1	1	1	1	1
General dysfunctioning	2	–	–	–	2	–	2	–	2
Speech dysfunctioning	3	1	1	–	1	2	1	1	2
Sensory dysfunctioning	3	1	1	1	–	2	1	2	1
Cognitive dysfunctioning	9	2	4	2	1	6	3	4	5
Obsessive thoughts	2	–	–	1	1	–	2	1	1
Random activity	2	–	–	2	–	–	2	2	–

	1	2	3	4	5	6	7	8	9
Enhanced strength	9	6	3	—	—	9	—	6	3
General discomfort	12	4	4	3	1	8	4	7	5
Heat, fever	3	1	1	1	—	2	1	2	1
Cold	1	1	—	—	—	1	—	1	—
Tension	1	1	—	—	—	1	—	1	—
Negative attitudes toward world, future	7	2	1	1	3	3	4	3	4
Expressive behavior: Smile, laugh	1	—	—	1	—	—	1	1	—
Expressive behavior: Crying	21	4	6	5	6	10	11	9	12
Loss of self-awareness	2	1	1	—	—	2	—	1	1
Not eat	6	—	1	3	2	1	5	3	3
Other feelings: Sadness, depression	2	—	1	—	1	1	1	—	2
SITUATIONS									
Aggression by adult	20	5	6	3	6	11	9	8	12
Aggression by child	22	5	4	10	3	9	13	15	7
Other	4	1	2	—	1	3	1	1	3
Not specified	14	4	3	2	5	7	7	6	8

Table 4. The Subjects Participating in the Study of Productive Thinking

	Subject	Age	Term	Occupation of Parent or Guardian
Older Boys				
in English	1	14	P−7	Policeman
	2	14	P−7	Driver
	3	14	P−7	Watchman
	4	14	P−7	Shopkeeper
	5	14	P−7	Cashier
Older Boys				
in Luganda	6	14	P−7	Farmer
	7	14	P−7	Headman
	8	14	P−7	Shopkeeper
	9	14	P−7	Shopkeeper
	10	14	P−7	Shopkeeper
Older Girls				
in English	11	14	P−7	Ayah
	12	13	P−7	Nurse
	13	13	P−7	Shopkeeper
	14	14	P−7	Local Chief
	15	14	P−7	Trader
Older Girls				
in Luganda	16	14	P−7	Salesman
	17	14	P−7	Tradesman
	18	14	P−7	Trader
	19	14	P−7	Clerk
	20	14	P−7	Trader
Younger Boys				
in Luganda	21	10	P−3	
	22	11	P−6	Butcher
	23	11	P−6	Doctor
	24	11	P−6	Trader
	25	11	P−6	Farmer
Younger Girls				
in Luganda	26	11	P−7	Trader
	27	10	P−6	Tailor
	28	11	P−6	Shopkeeper
	29	10	P−6	Driver
	30	11	P−5	

Table 5. Median Score Per Item and Range of Scores for
Each Subgroup on Each Subtest

		Instances	Uses	Similarities	Patterns	Lines
Older Boys In Luganda	Median	5.7	5.2	5.2	3.2	3.4
	Range	3.7–13.0	4.5–9.2	4.4–8.4	2.0–5.0	2.6–6.2
Older Girls in Luganda	Median	6.3	5.8	5.2	2.4	2.6
	Range	5.7–8.0	3.0–8.8	3.0–5.6	1.0–4.2	1.4–7.0
Older Boys in English	Median	8.0	5.0	5.2	4.6	4.0
	Range	4.7–18.0	3.0–10.8	1.6–9.8	0.4–5.4	2.2–7.2
Older Girls in English	Median	5.3	4.3	3.2	2.8	3.4
	Range	1.7–8.3	2.5–8.0	1.8–3.8	1.2–5.0	2.0–4.6
Younger Boys in Luganda	Median	7.7	6.8	4.8	3.8	3.6
	Range	4.7–12.0	3.0–6.8	0.8–5.2	2.2–5.2	2.0–8.0
Younger Girls in Luganda	Median	3.7	3.8	3.2	2.6	2.2
	Range	2.0–6.3	2.0–6.0	1.6–4.4	2.0–4.2	2.0–3.2

Table 6. Median Scores and Ranges on Each Subtest for Older
and Younger Groups in English and Luganda

		Instances	Uses	Similari- ties	Patterns	Lines
Older in Luganda	Median	6.2	5.5	5.2	2.9	3.1
	Range	3.7–13.0	3.0–9.2	3.0–8.4	1.0–5.0	1.4–7.0
Older in English	Median	6.3	4.8	3.3	3.7	3.7
	Range	1.7–18.0	2.5–10.8	1.6–9.8	0.4–5.4	2.0–7.2
Younger in Luganda	Median	6.0	4.8	3.8	3.2	3.1
	Range	2.0–12.0	2.0–6.8	0.8–5.2	2.0–5.2	2.0–8.0

III

Pupils' Perceptions of the School as a System

MARY ALICE WHITE

This exploratory study[1] attempted to assess certain perceptions of pupils in a Uganda sample, and to compare these perceptions with those of a sample of 3,500 pupils in the schools in the Middle Atlantic region of the United States.[2] This was the broad question posed: Do pupils, regardless of culture or country, tend to read the school as a system in similar ways? A second question involved an attempt to identify those perceptions which might be particular to the Uganda sample and which might have educational implications.

SAMPLING AND PROCEDURAL LIMITATIONS

It must be made very clear from the outset that any inferences from this sample have to be viewed with considerable caution. Three of the investigators (C. Kimball, K. Kimball, and the writer) were unfamiliar with Ugandan schools and culture and did not speak Luganda. Undoubtedly they seemed strange to the pupils in many ways, apart from the restraints imposed by an American accent. Two research associates (Mr. Abbey Kibalama and Miss Rachel Lutu) worked with pupils in Luganda and in Swahili, so that it was possible to make comparisons of the material in terms of vernacular versus English. However, the sample itself certainly was not representative of all Ugandan schools and pupils. The sample was limited to schools within a fifty-mile radius of Kampala; and although every attempt was made to select a wide range of schools, such representation may not have been achieved. These were the participating schools:

Kibuli Primary School
Kiswera Primary School
Luzira Primary School
Makerere Hill Primary School
Naguru-Katali

Nakasero Primary School
Nakivubo Settlement School
Nkozi Primary School
Nsangi School

In selecting the pupils from each class, the same method of random selection was employed as had been used in earlier work in the United States. The classroom was divided into hypothetical quarters, and a boy or girl was chosen alternately and at random from within each quarter. Presumably this assured a fairly random selection over a large number of classes.

The technique used with the pupils may have presented some special language and cultural problems in this sample. The technique, which had been developed in the U.S. sample and termed "teaching exchanges," consists of asking a pair of pupils from one grade to teach a subject to a pair of pupils from the next lower grade. The technique has permitted study of the ways in which pupils spontaneously teach each other, their choices of material from the curriculum, and their perceptions of the important aspects of school. In using this technique with Ugandan pupils, one problem resulted from having some of the older pupils work in English when their command of it was not complete, thereby creating some stilted and restricted use of language. The other main problem, which occurred both with the American investigators and with the African investigators working in the vernacular, was the shyness of the pupils in talking spontaneously in front of an adult. This is strikingly different from the American sample, where spontaneity between the pupils was easily established, allowing the children to carry on a natural conversation among themselves while an adult took notes. It is very hard to assess the relative roles of language facility, age, and shyness. The younger pupils in P-3 and P-4 appeared more spontaneous, perhaps because of their age, but also perhaps because they were working in the vernacular.

The total sample is described in Table 1 by primary level and sex. Only pupils from P-3 through P-7 were sampled, in order to select age ranges comparable to the earlier U.S. sample. The total sample included 306 pupils, of whom 142 were boys and 164 were girls. Tables 2 and 3 describe the sample by stream and by language employed in data collection.

RESULTS

A majority of the pupils were asked to teach what they thought were their most important subjects. Table 4 reports their opinions by primary level. It is quite clear that mathematics and English stand out even among the younger pupils and are clearly predominant by P-6 and P-7. It would be reasonable to assume that much of the emphasis on these two subjects stems from the P-7 examination, in which mathematics and English are heavily stressed.

However, we wished to compare these perceptions with those of the U.S. sample, where we had found that the amount of homework and the frequency of tests were associated with pupils' perceptions of what was important to learn in school. Consequently, we used a subsample within the same schools to inquire about homework and tests. The results, shown in Tables 5 and 6, are similar to those for the U.S. sample in this regard, as the choice of important subjects appears to coincide with the reported work load, namely homework and tests. This is not to deny that the emphasis within the curriculum, including the amount of homework and testing, is very likely to be a conscious preparation for the P-7 examinations. But it is of some interest to see that this sample appears to follow what we have found to be broadly true within the U.S. sample, that pupils respond to work load as an indicator of what pupils assume to be important in school.

The system of rewards and punishments utilized within the school, as reported by these children (the same subsample that provided the data for Tables 5 and 6), is summarized in Table 7 in simple frequency counts. In Parts A and B, reported negative and positive actions and corresponding school responses are shown; in Part C, reported negative actions for which no corresponding school action was cited; and in Part D, reported school punishments for which no corresponding negative action was cited.

Although the material in Table 7 is very limited, it does suggest that the action-response system of the schools in this sample is clearly perceived by the pupils. In their verbal reports this was even more evident, for the pupils spoke without hesitation, and with sureness, of exactly what would happen in their particular school if a pupil did a certain thing. Referring again to Table 7, we see, too, that reported school responses to negative actions ($N = 62$) were more numerous than reported responses to positive actions ($N = 22$). This was also true of the U.S. sample, even though the action-response system is quite different in the United States. We might speculate that pupils tend to perceive the punishment aspects of a school system much more clearly than they do the rewards, or that the school as a system has many more visible and frequent punishments than it does rewards.

Another aspect of Table 7 worth mentioning is the nature of the rewards and punishments which are reported. Bearing in mind the small sample and its possible lack of representation, we still might pause over the implications of punishments associated with agricultural labor. We note the use of slashing grass, digging, cutting reeds, fetching water, and cleaning the compound, as punishments for being lazy, for fighting, or other misdemeanors. Assuming that agriculture will have to play a major role in the Ugandan economy for some time to come, one might wonder whether such work can be held in esteem by pupils when it is imposed as punishment for laziness or misbehavior. Further, there was no reported instance of such agricultural punishments being used in response to poor academic work. The reported school reaction to this appears to be corporal punishment, detention, repetition of work, chastisement by the teacher, or loss of position in the academic pecking order of the school.

An over-all view of the data in Table 7 suggests that the hierarchy of school behavior is based upon being a good student, and behaving well within the explicit rules of the school. These are rewarded by the school, as indicated in Part B. However, the value of good scholarship and good behavior was so clearly perceived by the pupils in terms of their own cultural mores, and the rewards further education could bring, that further emphasis by the school might not be necessary. Later, when we discuss Table 9, regarding parental responses to child behavior, we shall see an interesting correspondence between school and family values.

Another way of assessing how clearly pupils understand the school as a system is to see how well they agree on the meaning of the symbols used as marks. Our findings about this are summarized in Table 8. In the schools sampled, all individual subjects were marked on a numerical scale from zero to one hundred. In addition, marks were added for a total score on the term report, and also added for a total score on the P-7 exam. A substantial degree of agreement within a subsample is shown in Table 9 for the pupils' numerical values for "a high mark," "an average mark," and "a low mark." This agreement is partially due to the uniformity of the marking system from school to school and from subject to subject. But it can also be said that the pupils themselves, even at these young ages, appear to have a reasonably clear and consistent notion of what the marks symbolize in the way of academic performance. This is in great contrast with our findings for the U.S. sample, where we found considerable confusion among similar age pupils as to the meaning of marks. This is partly due to the tendency in the United States to use a variety of marking systems between schools and between grade levels, which results in considerable confusion in the pupil's mind as to the evaluation of his work. In the present Uganda sample, it is clear that marks are extremely important to the pupil's future opportunity for further education and employment. It is therefore considered an advantage by this writer that the marking system appears so clearly understood.

Now we turn to the pupils' descriptions of parental response to school performance, shown in Table 9, so that we can assess the correspondence between school and family response to schooling. We observe that the responses reported for the parent are unequivocal and quite discriminating between poor and good school reports. Corporal punishment, as well as removal from school, is anticipated in the event of a poor report. A good report seems to be far better rewarded at home than it is in school, with parents apparently giving their children presents and prizes in most instances. We note again, as we did in reference to Table 7, that agricultural punishments are employed occasionally for poor school performance. The overriding impression from Table 9 is that the parental rewards and punishments are not only clear but quite consistent with the system used by the school. The ultimate danger is that the pupil will not be allowed to *continue* his schooling. To anyone familiar with the school system in the United States, the disparity between the two samples in this matter is both obvious and enormous. One cannot equate parental responses in a universal public compulsory educational system to those in a selective and highly competitive one. Although we have very meager data on this for the U.S. sample, it is unlikely that the parental threat of not being allowed to attend school would come into the picture at all in the United States; nor would the role of the cost of education be so great.

In Table 10, the pupils' reports of how they determine their academic progress in school are summarized. It should be clear here, as it was in listening to the pupils, that the copybook, or exercise book, is the constant source of measurement of how well one is doing. This comes in two forms: the written comments of the teacher, either positive or negative, as shown in item 1 in Table 10; and the work marked correct or to be repeated, as shown in item 2 in Table 10. Thus there is both a qualitative evaluation, provided by the written comments of the teacher, and a quantitative evaluation, indicated by the amount of work to be done. In some schools the pupils reported that their copybooks were studied during a study period; in others they reported that their copybooks were also carried home each afternoon. It appears that the copybook acts as a constant reference for each pupil's progress, as well as a source of the material which needs further study or correction.

What is not clear, either in the pupils' explanations or in the limited data shown in Table 10, is the role of explanation of the source of error. Both in Luganda and in English, we found it very hard to ascertain the frequency of explanation which occurs between the teacher and a pupil when an error is made at the blackboard, in the copybook, or in class recitation. In some instances, pupils reported that they could receive individual help from the teacher during study period or during class, but in other instances, we had the impression that pupils would be reluctant to ask for help (as a display of ignorance) or that any explanation would be directed to the class as a whole. The role of explanation will be discussed further when we describe the nature of the teaching exchanges.

Tables 11, 12, and 13 represent special areas of interest which we decided to explore midway through our collection of our data when we found ourselves puzzled by certain questions. One question was: Do pupils in the sample schools have a high level of vocational aspiration? This had been our impression, based on what we had heard during the teaching exchanges. Table 11 summarizes the data for a small subsample of 70 pupils. Before inferring anything from such answers, one must be cautious in evaluating the vocational aims which children state. In the U.S. sample, we have noticed that pupils tend to report vocational aims that represent wishes more than realities, as well as vocational goals which they feel will be acceptable to their peers and to adults. On the other hand, such fantasy (if it is that) has a certain validity in suggesting what children believe to be desirable, if not realistic. Some of the pupils whose goals are reported in Table 11 added that they doubted their ability to realize them, saying, for example, "But my future is uncertain. If I have luck I should like to be a ____, but my father is poor and cannot afford secondary school, so perhaps I shall be a farmer."

With these cautions in mind, one may read Table 11 as a small sample of aspirations, if not of realistic goals. Over half of the responses in Table 11 demonstrate vocational goals which are professional in nature (doctor, nurse, teacher). Such goals represent a large investment in educational fees, plus the ability to succeed in a highly competitive and selective school system at higher levels. The choices of some of the younger children (driving a tractor, being a conductor, being a mechanic) may represent particular interests of children of this age, and this is equally true of the U.S. sample, rather than mature vocational goals. However, assuming that the very limited data shown in Table 11 are some indication of what a sample of school children in Uganda would like to achieve, one might be concerned about the possible discrepancy between their wishes and the likelihood of their realization. Judging from the economic forecasts,[2] the probability of this proportion (65 per cent) of professional occupations being absorbed into the Ugandan economy in the near future seems very slim indeed. The discrepancy between their aspirations and reality may become a source of disquiet to this emerging generation of pupils. The more realistic goal within the economy seems to be agriculture, which only 3 of these 70 pupils elected—and, as might be expected, these came from rural schools. We notice also that some of the goals expressed (pilot, air hostess) are the glamour jobs of the jet age.

What appears to be lacking is a fit between what will be possible within the Ugandan economy for this generation of primary school pupils, and what they desire. This lack of fit may be especially significant because these 70 children constitute a highly selective sample of all school children in Uganda. One might assume that, precisely because they are already selective, those fortunate enough to attend school through Primary-7 may have higher aspirations which are more likely to be realized. But we must also recognize that only approximately 5 to 10 per cent of those shown in Table 11 can expect to find openings in secondary school. Without admission to secondary, at least half of the 15 vocations listed in Table 11 would be impossible to pursue.

The second question we had a particular interest in exploring was the role of language in the daily lives of these pupils. In the teaching exchanges, we had noted a lack of verbal fluency which, as mentioned earlier, we attributed to cultural shyness with adults, since it seemed to occur equally in Luganda and in English. We wondered whether these pupils talked with each other, or with members of their families, about the cognitive material covered in school. In an attempt to get at this question indirectly, we recorded the daily sequential schedules of 137 pupils and tallied the activities mentioned therein, as shown in Table 12. These data are essentially repetitive, and may only indicate what these pupils see as the events worth reporting to an adult. Inspection of Table 12 shows the important roles of eating, washing, chores, prayers, free play, and walking to and from school. One gets the impression that there is relatively little time for educational pursuits at home, because of the time spent in doing chores, such as fetching water and caring for younger children, and in walking to school, which means long distances in the rural area. To what extent the reports of reading and studying are reliable is very hard to estimate, especially since such activities would require the expense of a lamp. The radio is apparently listened to by most families and was the basis upon which we could estimate time for many of the evening activities. What may be of more interest in this table is what was *not* spontaneously reported: *no* pupil spontaneously mentioned conversation with parents or siblings, and the item "conversation with peers" appears only because we specifically asked about it. This does not mean that these children do not talk to each other, however, for even the most casual observation during break or on the playground suggests that they chatter as vivaciously as any group of school children do. What is suggested is that their practice in language fluency may be restricted in terms of child-adult interchange, particularly in regard to the cognitive content of their school learning.

After the schedules of the 137 children had been recorded, we made specific inquiries of 51 of these same children about the content of their conversation with peers. Their answers are summarized in Table 13. When we specifically asked about the content of conversation walking to and from school with peers and siblings, we were most often told that school work was the leading topic of conversation. This was true both in Luganda and in English. It is very hard, once again, to evaluate what was being said in front of adults for their benefit, versus what actually occurs on such walks. Many of the topics mentioned are commonly of interest to children, such as who was punished in school today, accidents, food, games, and so on; but the emphasis reported on school work seems unduly high. If these reports are accurate, we must assume that there is considerable use of language among peers to describe what is being learned, and that among themselves these pupils may discuss problems in school learning in fluent fashion. We asked a small subsample of children to tell us who helped them with their homework. Among 20 children, 12 indicated that their older siblings helped them, 4 indicated their parents, and 4 reported no resource. None named their teacher, but perhaps they interpreted the question to mean help at home.

We have no definitive answer to the questions we raised about the use of language to facilitate learning. On the one hand, it is quite possible that among themselves, and in the absence of any adult, the children may use language frequently and fluently to discuss cognitive school material. On the other hand, there may be infrequent use of language between child and adult in these cognitive areas, due in part at least to the quiet and subdued role the children in this culture are expected to assume. It was because of certain observations made during the teaching exchanges that we had made further inquiry into language usage, so we turn now to discussion of the teaching exchanges themselves.

THE TEACHING EXCHANGES

As compared to the teaching exchanges in the U.S. sample, the outstanding difference was the lack of spontaneous language in the Ugandan sample. This may well be due to the cultural shyness of children before adults, but we would like to point out some specific areas where the pupils appeared to lack certain techniques for furthering their learning.

When the pupils started to teach each other, they began without explanation, which was also true of the U.S. sample. These pupils taught, however, in ways we would term stilted. Their technique was limited almost entirely to demonstration and repetition, if it were in mathematics, or to a statement followed by a question calling for repetition of the statement, if it were in another subject. In English, they would pronounce a rule and then ask the other pupils to repeat the rule. The use of examples was particularly interesting, for the pupils appeared either to have a limited repertoire of examples, or else they preferred to use examples which were very much alike. In mathematics, for example, a pupil would give one problem or sum to the children to do, followed by other problems which were exactly alike in their construction and varying only slightly in their values.

We also noticed that the pupil in the role of the teacher rarely indicated whether a pupil's answer was correct or incorrect. The spoken answers were met with silence, unless the adult investigator interviewed to ask for a reaction. We would hypothesize that there was inadequate feedback for maximal learning.

The pupils as teachers seemed to stress the correct operation rather than the principle. For example, if each step in finding the area of a triangle was not written on a separate line, the pupil-teacher would insist that it be done over again, without attending to whether or not the child had understood the operations required. Quite often the only technique employed to correct an error was for the pupil-teacher to redo the example himself for the presumed benefit of the child who had made the error.

In the younger age groups, working in Luganda, there were more questions of "why" and more demands for explanation. From P-5 up, it appeared that what was taught was unquestioned. This may be due to overlapping in the curriculum, for often it appeared that the pupils had already been exposed to the material being taught and therefore would be unlikely to raise questions about it.

In a few instances, we tried to explore the pupils' understanding of proof in its scientific sense, versus proof based on authority. The material is much too scanty to merit more than the impression that scientific proof did not appear to be well understood or highly regarded.

We also received the impression that in mathematics the pupils seemed to have more difficulty with numerical operations than with formulas. They had mastered the formulas, but were often unable to solve a given problem at the P-7 and P-6 level which called for 15 divided by 2, or 300 divided by 6. Their answers were wrong, but the pupil-teacher in almost every instance seemed not to recognize the source of the error and would require the whole problem to be done over again. Compared to the U.S. sample of similar ages, there was less tendency on the part of the pupil-teacher to locate the source of the error.

Assuming that these observations from the teaching exchanges have some limited validity, what inferences may we draw? It is not necessarily relevant to compare this sample's learning and teaching techniques with a U.S. sample. One apparent difference is the use of language itself as a vehicle for learning, but this is so tied to cultural differences that the comparison may be inappropriate. In this exploratory study we made no systematic observations of classroom teaching, so one obvious question left unanswered is: To what extent are the teaching techniques an imitation of classroom teaching? We had the impression that the pupils often were imitating their teachers in employing a didactic method, addressed to the whole class, in which drill was the major method used. Whether these are the most appropriate teaching techniques for the available teaching staff and for their pupils is beyond our competence to judge.

GENERAL IMPRESSIONS

The data gathered in this exploratory study suggest:

1. That the school as a system is clearly understood by the pupils in terms of what the school stresses in its curriculum, in its marking system, and in its rewards and punishments.

2. That the reward-and-punishment system of the home, as it relates to school learning, is very consistent with that of the school.

3. That a high value is placed upon vocational goals requiring higher education, with little value placed on agricultural occupations. This same

value system seems to be reflected in the reward-and-punishment systems of school and home. This value system seems inconsistent with the probable future trends of the economy.

4. That the pupils appear to have a limited repertoire of learning techniques. There are many possible explanations for this, in terms of culture, language fluency, and classroom practices.

5. That the school, as a system, is clear and consistent in the eyes of its pupils. The only question that might be raised in this regard is the limited number who can succeed within such a system and the possible lack of alternatives for those who do not, whose aspirations may be equally high.

6. Assuming a primarily agricultural economy and limited educational resources, a somewhat better fit between the two may become crucial. This would imply a major change in the current value system, possibly through alteration of the rewards and punishments currently utilized in school and at home, in types of educational opportunity, and in economic advancement.

Table 1. Characteristics of Sample by Primary Level and Sex

	Boys	Girls	Total
P–7	39	46	85
P–6	37	47	84
P–5	21	23	44
P–4	24	26	51
P–3	20	22	42
	142 +	164 =	306

Table 2. Description of Sample by Streaming

	Boys	Girls
One stream only	63	72
Stream A (of 2 streams)	22	31
Stream B (of 2 streams)	25	29
Stream (x or D)	2	2
Streamed by age	2	2
Heterogeneous streaming	28	28
	142	164

Table 3. Language Employed in Data Collection

	Boys	Girls
English	83	89
Luganda	49	52
Luganda and English	8	21
Swahili	2	2
	142	164

Table 4. Subjects Reported as Most Important by Primary Level

	P–7	P–6	P–5	P–4	P–3	Total
Mathematics	21	23	20	20	9	93
English	40	19	8	15	4	86
Geography	–	2	3	1	2	8
History	2	1	1	–	1	5
Science	–	1	–	2	–	3
Music	–	–	1	2	–	3
Religion	–	–	1	–	1	2
	63	46	34	40	17	200

Table 5. Subjects in Which Most Homework Was Reported

	Boys	Girls
Math	25	29
English	13	19
History	2	2
	40	50

Table 6. Subjects in Which Most Tests Were Reported

	Boys	Girls
Math	26	27
English	24	24
Science	1	1
Geography	1	–
	52	52

Table 7. Perceived System of School Rewards and Punishments

A. NEGATIVE ACTION AND SCHOOL RESPONSE

Negative Action	Perceived School Response	N
being lazy	beating	3
	detention	2
	kneeling down	1
	miss a meal	1
	send you home	1
	slash grass	1
	digging	1
	cutting reeds	1
	cleaning compounds	1
	fetching water	1
		13
low marks	beating	4
	extra school work	3
	detention	2
	kneeling down	1
	sent out of class	1
	moved down a stream	1
	teacher talks to you	1
	headmaster sends you home	1
	correct work at blackboard	1
	teacher not pleased	1
	do corrections	1
	send you away (expelled)	1
		18
fighting	beating	10
	fetching water	3
	cleaning school	2
	slashing grass	2
	digging	1
	sent out of class	1
	dismissed from school	1
	letter sent home	1
		21
insulting teacher	send you out of school	2
	headmaster beats me	1
		3

Table 7. Perceived System of School Rewards and Punishments—*(Cont'd.)*

A. NEGATIVE ACTION AND SCHOOL RESPONSE—*(Cont'd.)*

Negative Action	*Perceived School Response*	*N*
speaking in class	take away your stars	1
playing in class	detention	1
	stand outside class	1
		2
stealing	parents come to school and beat them 10 sticks	1
	sent out of school	1
		2
harming school property	detention	1
	whipping	1
		2
Total School Responses Reported for Negative Actions		62

B. POSITIVE ACTION AND SCHOOL RESPONSE

Positive Action	*Perceived School Response*	*N*
doing well in schoolwork	school gives presents	12
	given stars	3
	given cup	1
	given book tokens	1
		17
being clean	given soap and basin	1
good behavior	given stars	1
good at sports	team cup and badge	1
good written composition	read before whole school	1
looking after other children	given plate	1
Total School Responses Reported for Positive Actions		22

Table 7. Perceived System of School Rewards and Punishments—*(Cont'd.)*

C. NEGATIVE ACTIONS REPORTED WITHOUT REFERENCE TO SCHOOL RESPONSE

coming late to school (8)
disobedient (4)
throwing stones (4)
swinging on the bars (2)
failing to attend church (2)
insulting others (2)
breaking equipment

playing in church
revenging on others
hurting another pupil
running in corridor
climbing trees
failure to do homework
(not reported spontaneously,
   only upon inquiry)

D. SCHOOL PUNISHMENTS REPORTED WITHOUT REFERENCE TO NEGATIVE ACTIONS

digging (3)
slashing grass (2)
fetching water (2)
beatings (2)
holding up stones (2)

cutting reeds
cleaning compound
smearing cow-dung on floors
washing latrine
running around compound

Table 8. Reported Values of Marking System
(Range: 0–100)

	$\overline{X}$	S.D.
"High" (N = 35)	86	10.3
"Average" (N = 28)	47	8.3
"Low" (N = 18)	18	12.9

Table 9. Reported Parental Responses to
Children's School Performance

Nature of School Report	Reported Parental Response	N
poor school report	1. beat you, whip you	16
	2. take me out of school	7
	3. parents angry	4
	4. extra school work	3
	5. arrange for tutoring	3
	6. not give me any money	2
	7. no food	2
	8. digging	1
	9. work hard on farm	1
	10. lock in room	1
	11. say "waste our money"	1
		41
good report	1. parents give prizes, presents	21
	2. parents pleased	6
	3. parents thank you	4
	4. give me food	3
	5. parents love you	1
	6. give me clothes	1
	7. allow me to stay up late	1
		16
average report	1. tell me to work harder	1
misbehavior in school	1. beat you	2
	2. withhold food	2
	3. parents beg headmaster for you to stay in school	1
		5

Table 10. Perceived System of School Evaluation

	N
1. By teacher's written comments in copybook (Star, "good," "repeat," "poor or dirty," etc.)	44
2. By work in copybook (ticks, crosses, work repeated, etc.)	13
3. By marks	7
4. By test scores	6
5. By answering correctly in class	4
6. By reports at end of term	3
7. By being moved up or down in stream	2
8. By teacher whipping you	1
9. By teacher calling me to show me how to do the work	1
10. By headmaster writing special letter to parents	1
11. By parents coming to see headmaster	1
	83

Table 11. Reported Vocational Aspirations by Primary Level
(N = 70)

	P–7	P–6	P–5	P–4	P–3	Total
Doctor	4	5	4	3	2	18
Nurse	1	2	5	5	2	15
Teacher	2	2	1	4	3	12
Pilot	2	2	2	–	–	6
Mechanic	1	1	–	2	–	4
Policewoman	2	–	–	1	–	3
Farmer	1	1	–	–	1	3
Lawyer	–	1	–	–	1	2
Airport hostess	1	–	–	–	–	1
Secretary	1	–	–	–	–	1
Clerk	–	–	1	–	–	1
Typist	–	–	1	–	–	1
Shopkeeper	–	–	1	–	–	1
Conductor	–	–	–	1	–	1
Drive tractor	–	–	–	1	–	1
Total	15	14	15	17	9	70

Table 12. Reported Daily Activities
(*N* = 137 Schedules)

Activity	Number of Times Reported
Eating	240
Washing	128
Chores at home	111
Prayers	108
Free play	97
Walking to and from school	91
Greeting parents	88
Dressing	58
Reading (at home)	56
Conversation with peers (while walking to school)	45
Listening to radio	36
Studying (at home)	29
Buying food	20
Watching TV	10
Sleeping during day	5
Conversation with parents or siblings	0

Table 13. Reported Topics of Conversation with Peers
(*N* = 51)

Topic	Number of Pupils
School work	15
Future jobs	9
Punishments	5
Accidents	5
Food	4
Games	4
Siblings	2
Sports matches	2
Cars	2
Friends	2
Home affairs	1
	51

Conclusion:
Research in Teaching, Learning, and Human Development

At this point in the development of education in East Africa, the need for research relevant to problems of educational practice is certainly too obvious to belabor. In nearly every conference devoted to education in Africa, the imperative need for research dealing with realistic and practical issues in education has been emphasized.

In the rapidly developing countries of East Africa, educators face a wide variety of extraordinarily complex problems about which they must make decisions that have immediate as well as long-term impact on the development of East Africa. Currently, these decisions are based largely on the opinions of "experts," on traditional practices, and on knowledge about teaching, learning, and human development derived from other cultures. From a pragmatic point of view, decisions have had to be made without waiting for research to be done. But now, after this initial period of rapid expansion of educational opportunities in East Africa, if effective and efficient decisions are to be made on a rational and realistic basis, the development of a systematic, rigorous body of knowledge directly relevant to problems actually encountered in the schools of East Africa is necessary.

This need—for a body of systematic information—clearly implies another: the need for research focused on concrete educational problems. Research questions should be derived from specific difficulties experienced by educators, and the results of research should have immediate feedback into the on-going process of education.

Nevertheless, it will be useful to formulate any investigation into the practical issues of education within a broader theoretical context of one or more of the disciplines related to education, such as psychology and sociology. The primary aim of the research should not be to test particular propositions derived from any specific theoretical framework, but to consider the theoretical context within which an investigation might best be formulated to enhance the interpretation and meaningfulness of results obtained. Therefore, in addition to the potential utilitarian value of such

71

research, there are also likely to be implications of more general theoretical interest.

While the principal immediate value of the research would be the feedback of results into the process of education, a most important auxiliary aspect would be the training of East African personnel in methods and procedures of educational research. There is currently a severe shortage of adequately trained investigators in this area, and the coordination of an on-going research project with on-the-job training of East African personnel will add a significant dimension to the final results of the research. East African students and scholars should have the opportunity to learn methods of empirical investigation.

In addition, teachers must themselves be involved in the process of research, so as to stimulate their interest in empirical investigation of educational problems, generate intellectual excitement about issues in education, and perhaps indirectly enhance their teaching skills through experience in techniques of observation and the logic of research thinking. The results of the 1967 Summer Project strongly support the likelihood of these kinds of positive side-effects.

Notes

I

1. This study owes its inspiration to Mr. Senteza Kajubi, Director of the Institute of Education, Makerere University College, Kampala. It became a reality through his interest and the active cooperation and participation of Messrs. T. Nsereko-Mussajagyagenda, B. Otaala, and J. Bigala, members of the Educational Psychology Department, Institute of Education, Makerere University College, Kampala. It received support from the Afro-Anglo-American Program in Teacher Education and the Center for Education in Africa, Institute of International Studies, of Teachers College, Columbia University. It was carried out during a six-week interval with the assistance of two students from the Institute of Education: Mr. L. Bombo and Miss P. Nakkazi. The children in the study were drawn from Kibuli Primary School (Mr. Mukasa, Headmaster) and Makerere Hill Primary School (Mr. Muwanga, Headmaster). Assistance in the beginning phases of the study was also provided by Mr. Lacey, Headmaster, Nakasero Primary School, and Mrs. M. Gumikiriza, Headmistress, Nakivubo Settlement Primary School. Their willingness to be questioned, and the special arrangements made by headmasters and teachers—arrangements helpful to us but often disruptive of normal routine—are much appreciated.

2. Barbel Inhelder and Jean Piaget, *The Early Growth of Logic in the Child* (New York: Harper and Row, 1964).

3. Benjamin Bloom, *Stability and Change in Human Characteristics* (New York: John Wiley and Sons, 1964).

4. Elizabeth Etuk, "The Development of Number Concepts: An Examination of Piaget's Theory with Yoruba Speaking Nigerian Children" (Unpublished Ed.D. dissertation, Teachers College, Columbia University, 1967).

5. Millie Almy with Edward Chittenden and Paula Miller, *Young Children's Thinking: Studies of Some Aspects of Piaget's Theory* (New York: Teachers College Press, 1966).

6. See *ibid.*, pp. 52–53, for a pictorial presentation of these tasks.

73

74

7. Inhelder and Piaget, *op. cit.*

8. Mr. E. Kiwanuka.

9. Almy, *op. cit.,* pp. 62–64.

10. *Ibid.*

11. See, for example, Roslyn Suchman, "Cultural Differences in Children's Color and Form Preferences," *Journal of Social Psychology,* 70 (1966), 3–10.

12. Ann Boehm, "The Development of Comparative Concepts in Primary School Children" (Unpublished Ph.D. dissertation, Columbia University, 1966).

13. Estelle Peisach, "The Relationship Between Language Usage and the Development of Conservation" (Unpublished Ph.D. dissertation, Columbia University, 1967).

14. For discussion of this point see Patricia Greenfield, "On Culture and Equivalence: II," in Jerome Bruner, *Studies in Cognitive Growth* (New York: John Wiley and Sons, 1966), pp. 270–318. Also Roslyn Suchman, *op. cit.*

II

1. Throughout this project, a number of people generously provided invaluable help, guidance, and support. In particular I wish to thank the following: Mr. W. Senteza Kajubi, Director of the Institute of Education, Makerere University College; Dr. Carl J. Manone, Chief of Party, AID/TEEA, and the members of his staff; Dr. A. Schelske, Mr. Nsereko-Musajjagyagenda, and Mr. Barnabas Otaala of the Institute of Education; Mr. Kabugo, Headmaster of Naguru/Katali Primary School; Mr. R. M. E. Lugumba, Headmaster of Makerere College Secondary School; Mr. Jackson Kaswa-Lyazi, Mr. J. E. Kasujja, and Mr. Pafula Kiwanuka, who served as research assistants; and Mrs. Judith Evans, the perfect coordinator of the project.

2. Michael A. Wallach and Nathan Kogan, *Modes of Thinking in Young Children: A Study of the Creativity-Intelligence Distinction* (New York: Holt, Rinehart and Winston, 1965).

III

1. The work which is reported here was carried out under the auspices of the Institute of Education, Makerere University, and its director, Mr. S. Kajubi, and was supported by Teachers College, Columbia University. The study was facilitated by the efforts and planning of the TEEA staff and its director, Dr. Carl Manone. The cooperation of the headmasters, staff, and pupils of the schools in our sample is gratefully acknowledged.

2. Studies of the American sample referred to in this monograph are reported in the following papers:

White, M. A. "The Child's World of Learning: Initial Explorations." 1965, mimeographed.

White, M. A. "Pupils' Perception of School Marks." *Elementary School Journal,* 67 (1967), 237–40.

White, M. A. "The View from the Pupil's Desk." *The Urban Review,* 2 (1968), No. 5, 5–7.

White, M. A., and Boehm, A. E. "Pupils' Discrimination of Important Ideas." Paper read at American Psychological Association, September, 1966.

White, M. A., and Boehm, A. E. "The Child's World of Learning: Written Workload of Pupils." *Psychology in the Schools,* 6 (1967), 70–73.

White, M. A., and Boehm, A. E. "Pupil versus Scholar." *Teachers College Record,* 69 (1968), 379–83.

3. *Work for Progress,* Uganda's Second Five-Year Plan (Entebbe, 1966).